Advance Praise for *The Bible's Yes to Same-Sex Marriage*

"In lucid, accessible prose, Mark Achtemeier makes plain what remains obscure for many: God's purposes for marriage, love, and sexuality according to the Bible. His book helps to clear away many harmful confusions, and it leaves in their place a rigorous sexual ethic that is both faithful to Scripture and inclusive of committed gay couples. It is an excellent introduction for those open to changing their position, and his witness is a worthy model to follow."

—Matthew Vines, founder of The Reformation Project
and author of *God and the Gay Christian*

"Many people experience a change in thinking when it comes to important matters of faith and life, but very few can articulate their transformation with careful clarity. Reading this book made me want to pull out some stationery and write Dr. Mark Achtemeier a long thank-you letter. I have such gratitude for Achtemeier's grace toward those who don't agree with him. I appreciate how he answers the questions that concern many loving Christians. And I admire him for taking the time to become a helpful guide for the church. Dr. Achtemeier's journey is not my journey, but throughout *The Bible's Yes to Same-Sex Marriage*, his perspective, thoughtfulness, and care moved and enlightened me."

—Carol Howard Merritt, pastor, columnist,
and author of *Tribal Church* and *Reframing Hope*

"For Christians who fear that embracing a gay-affirming theology means relinquishing biblical authority, Mark Achtemeier's careful, step-by-step exploration of the issue might prove an invaluable guide and comfort. This is no fiery treatise, no inflammatory polemic. This is a thoughtful, conservative theologian offering to hold the hand of the reader who cares to accompany him on his journey from the Christian he was to the Christian he is today."

—John Shore, founder of The Not All Like That (NALT)
Christians Project and author of *UNFAIR:
Christians and the LGBT Question*

"A deeply compelling read. I couldn't put it down. In these pages, an esteemed, conservative scholar shares his personal and theological journey through the complex terrain of the most divisive issue facing churches today. His method is solid, his humility is inspiring, and his insights are profound. I admire Mark Achtemeier's ability to tell a very human story about our place in the very holy Gospel story."

—Serene Jones, president of Union Theological Seminary, New York City, and author of *Trauma and Grace: Theology in a Ruptured World*

"With his skills as a distinguished biblical scholar, his pastor's heart, and his personal integrity, Mark Achtemeier carefully explores what Scripture says, and does not say, about same-sex relationships and marriage. This is the book we have been waiting for—biblically based, carefully researched, unapologetically Christ centered, and compellingly argued. It moved me deeply, and it will make an enormous contribution to the conversation in the church, and beyond, about one of the most important moral issues of our time."

—John M. Buchanan, editor/publisher of *The Christian Century*

The Bible's Yes
to Same-Sex Marriage

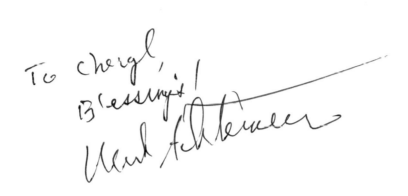

To Cheryl,
Blessings!
Mark Achtemeier

The Bible's Yes to Same-Sex Marriage

An Evangelical's Change of Heart

MARK ACHTEMEIER

WJK WESTMINSTER
JOHN KNOX PRESS
LOUISVILLE · KENTUCKY

First edition
Published by Westminster John Knox Press
Louisville, Kentucky

14 15 16 17 18 19 20 21 22 23—10 9 8 7 6 5 4 3 2 1

Book design by Drew Stevens
Cover design by Levan Fisher Design
Cover illustration: Bible © *DNY59/istockphoto.com*

Library of Congress Cataloging-in-Publication Data

Achtemeier, Mark, 1955-
   The Bible's yes to same-sex marriage : an evangelical's change of heart / Mark Achtemeier. -- First edition.
      pages cm
   ISBN 978-0-664-23990-9 (alk. paper)
1. Same-sex marriage--Religious aspects--Christianity. 2. Sex--Biblical teaching.
3. Homosexuality--Biblical teaching. 4. Marriage--Biblical teaching. I. Title.
   BT707.6.A24 2014
   241'.63--dc23

                                                                    2014009138

Most Westminster John Knox Press books are available at special quantity discounts
when purchased in bulk by corporations, organizations, and special-interest groups.
For more information, please e-mail SpecialSales@wjkbooks.com.

To my dear wife, Katherine,
beloved partner and companion on the journey

CONTENTS

ACKNOWLEDGMENTS

No writer works in a vacuum. Each of us is a product of the people, communities, institutions, and larger societies that have formed us into the persons we are. The important influences that have shaped me for the writing of this book are more than I can number. I would, however, like to acknowledge a particular debt of gratitude to the following:

To my wife, Katherine; my children, Rachel, Sarah, and Joshua; and my sons-in-law, Matt and Taylor, whose love, support, and enthusiasm for this project have sustained me through all of life's joys and struggles; to the leadership of Westminster John Knox Press for their encouragement to undertake this project; to my editor, David Maxwell, whose gentle encouragement and unflagging support have been of immense help in bringing this book to completion; to the congregation of First Presbyterian Church, Dubuque, Iowa, which has nurtured me in a community of vibrant engagement with the Scriptures; to the University of Dubuque Theological Seminary, which for many years provided an environment in which the thinking behind this book could take shape; to the Covenant Network of Presbyterians, which extended to me a brave welcome and sustaining hospitality at a time when my work had alienated me from former communities of support within the church; and finally, to the many members of the LGBT community who have shared with me your lives, your struggles, your aspirations, and most of all your friendship. You know who you are.

INTRODUCTION

This book is the story of a change of heart. In the middle 1990s, I was a conservative church activist working hard to defend the "traditional" teaching of my own Presbyterian Church (U.S.A.) that was condemning homosexual practice. In the fall of 1996, I published an article supporting traditionalist efforts to keep openly gay and lesbian people from serving in positions of ordained church leadership.[1] Those efforts proved successful, and the result was a constitutional ban on gay ordination in the Presbyterian Church (U.S.A.), beginning in the summer of 1997.[2]

The passage of fourteen years found me working to repeal the ban on gay ordination I had once helped put in place. My own efforts came to fruition, along with the work of a great many others, when on July 10, 2011, the PC(USA) officially repealed the constitutional language that had prevented faithful gay and lesbian Presbyterians from serving as ministers, elders, and deacons of the church. On October 8 of that year I was privileged to preach the sermon for the ordination of Scott Anderson, the first openly gay Presbyterian to be granted ministerial credentials under the new rules.[3]

The following pages chronicle the journey with the Bible that took me from a personal stance of judgment and exclusion to a changed heart that longs for the day when the church will fully celebrate and participate in God's blessing of same-gender relationships.

The Bible has been my constant guide and traveling companion on every step of this journey. Some people find this surprising: I remember speaking to a conservative Presbyterian who had heard about the change in my views. His first words upon meeting me were, "So when did you lose your faith?" It seems to be a common assumption that the only way a person could embrace this kind of a change would be to renounce the authority of Scripture or the Lordship of Christ, to decide that the Bible is outdated, or simply to ignore selected portions of scriptural teaching.

But nothing could be further from the truth! This journey for me has been a story of God leading and often prodding me into a steadily deepening encounter with Holy Scripture. My overriding goal has been to grapple honestly with this issue using the best principles of scriptural interpretation acquired through my work and training as a minister and theology professor. The result of this encounter with the Bible has been a growing conviction that the church's condemnation of same-gender relationships is a tragic and destructive misinterpretation of the Bible's message. Moreover it is a misinterpretation precisely because this so-called "traditional" teaching ignores classical principles of scriptural interpretation that date back centuries in the history of the church. Bringing these principles to bear on the question of same-gender relationships has led me to a deeper appreciation of the Bible's teaching in this area. The result has been not to undermine or ignore biblical teaching on love, sex, and marriage but to recognize how God's blessing is available to same-gender relationships just as much as to heterosexual ones.

Another thing people sometimes assume when they hear of this journey I have been on is that somewhere along the line I must have had a family member or loved one come out of the closet, or perhaps I have struggled with same-sex attraction myself. Again, the truth is quite different. God has blessed me with a wonderful marriage to my wife, Katherine, with whom I recently celebrated our thirty-second wedding anniversary. Together we have three wonderful children. We would love them as much as we do now if any of them happened to be gay, but none have shown any inclinations toward same-sex attraction.

This journey is not something I ever felt forced into. It began with some remarkable friendships that allowed me to catch a personal glimpse of the emotional and spiritual toll that the church's traditional condemnations were exacting on gay people who had a sincere desire to follow Jesus. Seeing the obstacles the church was putting in the way of their discipleship led me to wonder if the traditional condemnations against homosexuality contained problems that I had previously overlooked. The growing sense that something was wrong with this picture led me back to the Scriptures and set me out on this journey toward a more faithful and hopeful understanding of the Bible's message.

I believe that if the church attends carefully to the best biblical insights about marriage and sexuality from the Christian tradition, it will find that these teachings can open up rich possibilities for all Christian couples to experience God's blessing, whether their marriages are gay or straight. My goal has not been to overturn classical Christian teachings about marriage but to extend them so that their application to same-sex relationships becomes clear.

The time to make such a case is long overdue. I noted with alarm the results of a survey done a few years ago by the Barna research organization, which surveyed young people about their impressions of the church. The survey made national headlines when it found that eighty-five percent of unchurched young people thought of the Christian church as hypocritical, judgmental, and anti-gay.[4] As our society has become more aware of gay peoples' struggle for acceptance, the vocal opposition from many corners of the Christian community has led people outside the church to conclude that the

Bible and Christianity must inevitably function as sources of bigotry and exclusion.

These characterizations are not always fair. Having been a defender of the traditional, exclusionary teaching myself, I know that many people holding such views are convinced that same-gender sexual activity is a source of spiritual, emotional, and physical harm to the people who engage in it. Their oppositional stance is sometimes the product of an ill-informed compassion that seeks to prevent gay people from harming themselves.

But as the Barna survey makes clear, the presence of these good intentions has not been sufficient to allay the impression in the wider society that Christianity and the Bible are sources of hatefulness. This impression threatens to undermine the credibility of the church's witness for generations to come. It is high time for conscientious Christians to make the case that hatefulness and prejudice against gay people, far from reflecting the essence of Christianity, represent grave *distortions* of the Bible's message. Simply protesting the distortions will not be enough, however. To be credible, a critique of the distortions must be accompanied by a positive case for inclusion and acceptance based on a careful consideration of scriptural teaching.

I do hope what I have written here will prove helpful to gay people, as well as their families and friends who may be struggling to come to terms with who they are in the light of their Christian faith. I would, of course, like to persuade traditionalist Christians to change their views, and I trust that there are numbers among them for whom a carefully crafted biblical argument will be effective.

I have also encountered a great many compassionate and sympathetic Christian believers who hold traditionalist views but have a feeling deep in their hearts that something is not quite right with the church's exclusionary stance toward gay people. Many of these conscientious folk would like to support marriage equality but have felt uneasy about doing so in the absence of a clearly explained biblical case. I hope this record of my own journey will give them grounds for embracing in practice what their hearts already recognize as the right thing to do.

Though there is a great deal of excellent scholarship available on homosexuality and the Bible, I have not attempted with this work to provide a scholarly survey. Readers will find this book more of a spiritual travelogue, and my goal throughout has been to provide personal testimony to the discoveries that have kept me on the path of this remarkable journey. My actual progress has not been as direct or straightforward as the presentation of this book might indicate. I experienced many false starts and blind alleys along the way. But I do believe this work reflects an accurate chronicle of the biblical and intellectual milestones through which God has led me to this dramatic change of heart.

As I write these words, the Presbyterian Church (U.S.A.) continues to be in turmoil over questions of sexuality, in company with many other Christian denominations. The issue of gay marriage currently looms large on the agenda. The PC(USA) constitution presently prohibits Presbyterian ministers from performing wedding ceremonies for gay and lesbian couples, but challenges to this exclusionary stance will come before the church's General Assembly in the very near future. The arguments show no sign of abating, and it appears that American churches will be debating same-sex marriage for a long time to come. It is with the earnest hope of injecting some light into the midst of all the heat generated by these discussions that I have taken up the writing of this book.

CHAPTER 1

∞∞

THE HARVEST OF DESPAIR

Why Traditional Condemnations of Gay Relationships Can't Be Right

The young seminarian speaks to me in hushed tones across the table in the café where we have agreed to meet. Kristi (not her real name) is bright, capable, and committed, but today her face appears deeply troubled.

Kristi describes herself as a conservative evangelical who has always been deeply committed to Christ and the church. She has grown up convinced that God was calling her into full-time ministry, and she arrived at seminary tremendously excited about having her call become a reality.

Kristi also confesses to me that she has struggled with same-sex attraction since the time when she was a young teen. When she first became aware of these feelings she was horrified. At first she tried her best to ignore them, hoping they were a passing phase. But even though she never acted on them, the feelings have persisted over the years, becoming an ever deeper source of anguish and struggle for her.

I note the quaver in her voice as she speaks about all the years she has spent in fervent prayer, begging God to relieve her of what she believes are unholy impulses. She has sought out ministers and chaplains and Christian counselors. All have advised her to keep praying and hanging on, trusting that God will give her the strength to overcome these feelings.

As her story tumbles out, it becomes clear to me that Kristi is at the end of her rope. She speaks about faith with resentment in her voice, wondering why God would weigh her down with such an affliction when all she wants is to serve Christ as a committed disciple. She can't understand why a loving God would ignore her heartfelt prayers. She is not praying for any selfish reasons, she assures me, but only so that she can become the kind of faithful minister God has called her to be. After so much struggle, it is clear that God seems more like a distant, uncaring judge to Kristi than the loving, heavenly Father she grew up hearing about. Her future plans are in shambles, and she is on the verge of giving up on the faith altogether. The many years she has spent faithfully battling temptation and following church teaching have left her feeling bitter, hopeless, and deeply depressed. With tears running down her cheeks, she confesses to me she has been thinking about suicide.

I found Kristi's story very troubling, first and foremost on a human level because her deep distress couldn't help but tug at my heartstrings. But even beyond the emotional impact of her story, her testimony was disturbing because none of it matched up with the Bible's teaching about how faith and discipleship are supposed to work.

A really striking feature of Kristi's story was that through all this trial and struggle, she had continued to faithfully follow the path that her Christian mentors and teachers had identified as God's will for her life. This was not a story about a person falling prey to temptation and reaping a bitter reward as a result. Kristi had persisted in the battle against the troubling feelings that disturbed her so deeply. She had not surrendered to her impulses; she had done everything the church was telling her she should do. In many ways Kristi's struggle was a model of Christian faithfulness. Yet the result of this faithfulness was a depth of despair and brokenness that was very different from anything the Bible would lead us to expect.

Shouldn't Faithfulness Lead to Life?

The Bible is preoccupied from beginning to end with the choice between following God's will for us or falling away. And the consistent message that echoes throughout the pages of Scripture is that this choice—of being faithful to God or not—is a choice between life and death, light and darkness, hope and futility, flourishing and withering. Psalm 1 is absolutely typical as it describes the results of being faithful:

> Happy are those
>> who do not follow the advice of the wicked.
>
> . . . .
>
> but their delight is in the law of the Lord,
>> and on his law they meditate day and night.
> They are like trees
>> planted by streams of water,
> which yield their fruit in its season,
>> and their leaves do not wither.
> In all that they do, they prosper.
> The wicked are not so,
>> but are like chaff that the wind drives away.
>
> (Ps. 1:1–4)

Our loving God has set before us the path to life and blessing. Therefore we should choose life! This is the consistent message of Scripture.

But Kristi's story did not seem to fit this pattern at all. The result of her many years of faithful, costly obedience was not life and flourishing, but brokenness and spiritual exhaustion, alienation from God and a weariness that was leading her to give up on the faith altogether. These were not at all the outcomes Scripture would lead us to expect from a life of faithfulness.

This is not to suggest that faithfulness to Christ always leads to a peaceful life of serenity and comfort. The Bible never suggests that faithfulness will always be easy. Followers of Jesus are by no means exempt from facing hardship, suffering, and struggle in life, and in this they follow their Master's example. After all, the path of perfect faithfulness for Jesus led to the cross, and Christ teaches his followers that they, too, must be willing to pick up their crosses daily and follow him (Luke 9:23). God sometimes calls us to do things that are very hard for us.

But the Bible also speaks clearly and consistently about the blessing that attends such sacrifices in the form of closeness to God and the "peace of God, which surpasses all understanding" (Phil. 4:7). Jesus went to the cross out of his passionate desire to do the Father's will; as a result of his supreme sacrifice, God has highly exalted him (2:9–10). Paul and Silas, attacked by a hostile mob, beaten and thrown into prison, pass their time in captivity singing hymns of praise (Acts 16:16–25). The early Christian martyrs gave heartfelt testimony to God as they made the ultimate sacrifice for their faith. Even a modern-day martyr like Dietrich Bonhoeffer, imprisoned by the Nazis and struggling with isolation and depression in his filthy prison cell, gives a witness to a calm and sustaining faith that has inspired countless thousands down to the present day. A prison doctor gave the following eyewitness account of his death:

> Through the half-open door in one room of the huts I saw Pastor Bonhoeffer, before taking off his prison garb, kneeling on the floor praying fervently to his God. I was most deeply moved by the way this lovable man prayed, so devout and so certain that God heard his prayer. At the place of execution he again said a short prayer and then climbed the steps to the gallows, brave and composed. His death ensued after a few seconds. In the almost fifty years that I worked as a doctor, I have hardly ever seen a man die so entirely submissive to the will of God.[1]

The abiding presence of God, strengthening and upholding the faithful through times of hardship and suffering, has been a nearly universal feature of Christian experience from biblical times down to the present day.

But this was strikingly not the case for Kristi. The sacrificial commitments she had made in her attempts to remain faithful had resulted in alienation from God and loss of faith. I was left wondering: If this path Kristi had been walking produced results that were in so many ways the exact opposite of what Scripture would lead us to expect from a life of faithfulness, could it be that both she and I were mistaken about what path God really wanted her to follow?

Kristi's story didn't end there, but the events following our lunchtime conversation served only to reinforce my questions. By this point in my journey I had developed some contacts among gay Presbyterians. I was so concerned and shaken by the depth of Kristi's distress that I asked one of those friends if he might be willing to talk with her. That contact in turn put her in touch with a quiet fellowship of gay seminarians, many of whom had also come from very traditional backgrounds. These were people who had struggled with the same issues that had led Kristi to the brink of despair. Hearing their stories and becoming a part of their fellowship led Kristi for the first time to consider that God might not be automatically condemning her for the attractions she was feeling. For the first time she considered the possibility that her future might include sharing her life together with a partner whom she loved, in a relationship blessed by God.

The ensuing transformation in Kristi was remarkable. Her faith in God revived, stronger than ever. Her previous despair and depression rolled back, and a passionate, committed, Christ-centered young woman appeared, eager to be a witness of God's love. Once again, these were exactly the opposite results one would expect if her new openness was a move *away* from God's will for her. If a person's life departs in a serious way from God's will, one would not expect the result to be a flourishing spiritual commitment. John's Gospel records Jesus' clear teaching on this:

> I am the vine, you are the branches. Those who abide in me and I in them bear much fruit, because apart from me you can do nothing. Whoever does not abide in me is thrown away like a branch and withers. . . .
>
> (John 15:5–6)

Seeing Kristi's vibrant faith and strong commitment re-emerge as a result of her newfound openness made as deep an impression on me as her former despair. I couldn't help wondering if this really was the path God intended for her. I could see nothing in Kristi's life that looked like the spiritual withering one would expect to find in a person whose life had moved away from abiding in Christ.

Kristi's story is far from unique. I remember being struck early in my journey by the testimony of author and blogger Andrew Sullivan. Sullivan spoke in an interview about his early attempts to conform his life as a gay man to the teachings of his Roman Catholic faith, to which he was deeply devoted. Sullivan writes,

> The moral consequences, in my own life, of the refusal to allow myself to love another human being were disastrous. They made me permanently frustrated and angry and bitter. It spilled over into other areas of my life. Once that emotional blockage is removed, one's whole moral equilibrium can improve. . . . These things are part of a continuous moral whole. You can't ask someone to suppress what makes them whole as a human being and then to lead blameless lives. We are human beings, and we need love in our lives in order to love others, in order to be good Christians! What the church is asking gay people to do is not to be holy, but actually to be warped.[2]

Here again the same, puzzling pattern appears: Sullivan's committed attempts to follow church teaching on homosexuality did not lead to the spiritual flourishing that Scripture would lead us to expect as the fruit of true faithfulness. Instead they led to a spiritual life that was warped and stunted. Perhaps what the church was asking of gay people wasn't true faithfulness after all.

Another early conversation that got me thinking took place with a gay friend who was speaking to me about her marriage to her partner. I was suggesting, very generously I thought, that perhaps a commitment like hers could be justified from a Christian standpoint as a concession to human weakness: I believed that God's ideal for her as a gay person was to live a life of chaste singleness. But if she lacked the ability to do that, perhaps a marriage like hers could be viewed as a lesser evil in comparison with simply being promiscuous. Looking back on the conversation, I am amazed that she had the patience with me to respond in a civil manner, but her response has stayed with me. "I know all about sin and repentance," she said. "I have lots of areas in my life where I know I fall short and where I ask God's forgiveness and strive to do better. But my marriage just doesn't feel like one of these problem areas. My marriage feels like the part of my life that brings out the very best in me. It is where I learn the most about love and giving and self-sacrifice." Here was another striking break in the biblically predicted pattern: Scripture says that departing from God's will leads to spiritual withering. But the part of this person's life that I assumed was deeply contrary to God's will turned out to be one of the most fruitful areas of spiritual growth for her.

This conversation also started me wondering about what the church was asking gay people to do who were in committed, covenanted partnerships or marriages. Was it really God's will for people like my friend to abandon a beloved life partner and get a divorce?

I tried to think if there was any precedent in the Bible where God actively commands people to divorce their spouses. The one example I came up with was from Ezra, chapters 9–10. That biblical book chronicles the rebuilding of the nation of Israel following the peoples' return from seventy years in foreign exile. As chapter 9 opens, a group of officials brings to Ezra's attention a situation that has developed during the time of exile. Within that situation of captivity, many of the scattered Israelite men had intermarried with women from idol-worshiping foreign peoples, in violation of the Law of Moses. When Ezra and the other officials bring this situation to light, a great zeal for purifying their national life overtakes the Israelite masses. They resolve to "send away" their foreign wives and children, and the officials subsequently put in place a systematic plan for imposing divorces on all the affected families in the nation. The whole episode struck me as heartless and a bit chilling.

It is not at all clear that God approves of these mandatory divorces imposed on the nation. Nowhere in the story does anyone report a direct word from the Lord commanding this action; it is the idea of the religious leaders. Furthermore, the book of the prophet Malachi, which comes from the same period of Israel's history, contains a blistering condemnation of the divorces that have taken place within the nation (Mal. 2:13–16). This prophetic denunciation, which is reported as coming directly from God, sounds as if it is aimed squarely at this tragic episode of mandatory divorce undertaken by the returning exiles. The one recorded biblical instance where divorce is used as a remedy for marriages that were seen as violating God's law leads not to blessing but to divine judgment.

Finding no biblical precedent where divorce was required as an act of faithfulness, I tried to think about this situation from a personal standpoint as well. What would it be like to hear the church telling me that the only way my life could find favor in God's eyes would be for me to abandon my dear wife, Katherine, and seek a divorce? Whether or not I followed such teaching, what kind of damage would it do to my spiritual life and my view of God to hear a message like that coming from the church? I raised some of these questions in an address given to a gathering of conservative Presbyterians in 2002 and was surprised at the number of appreciative responses I received.[3]

As my circle of acquaintances within the gay community widened, I heard dozens of heartrending testimonies from committed gay Christians about the spiritual devastation that had resulted from desperately trying to conform their lives to the demands of a God whom they believed was standing in judgment over their longing for love and committed relationships.

And on the flip side of the ledger, I kept finding myself deeply impressed by the vibrant witness of gay Christians who had somehow come to terms with their sexual orientation and devoted themselves to following Jesus.

Sadly, I also encountered a great many stories that did not have the kind of happy ending I observed in Kristi's case. I became painfully aware of the thousands upon thousands of gay people who, upon finding themselves unable to live according to the requirements of traditional church teaching, had despaired of their faith, fled from the church, and lived under the assumption that the Christian God was their enemy. In the most heartbreaking cases, the burden of this spiritual devastation had proven too crushing to bear. These despairing children of God were turning to the path that had once tempted Kristi, seeing suicide as the only possible means of obtaining relief from the spiritual pain and heartbreak that resulted from their experiences with the church.

Asking the Impossible

My observations and experiences were raising a lot of questions about whether traditional church teaching on homosexuality was in accordance with God's will at all. As I became more and more aware of the personal and spiritual devastation that this teaching was causing, I realized that getting to the bottom of these questions was far more than just an intellectual exercise. Lives and souls were very much at stake. I had always assumed that the Bible's teaching on homosexuality was quite clear, but there was no denying the dramatic disconnect between the Bible's predictions about the fruits of faithfulness and the actual results I was seeing in the lives of gay people who followed, or tried to follow, this traditional teaching. I began wondering what I had overlooked in my own understanding of the Bible's teaching.

I also started to wonder what kind of God we were dealing with if the traditional condemnations of homosexuality really did reflect the will of God. These questions arose as I realized that people like Kristi did not choose their same-sex orientation, nor did they have the ability to embrace a lifelong discipline of celibate singleness.

It was absolutely clear from my conversations with Kristi and others that their sexual orientation was not a choice. Many of them had devoted years to prayer and struggle, pleading with God and desperately trying to be rid of their same-sex attraction, all to no avail. Scientists sometimes debate whether sexual orientation is determined by a person's genes or by external environmental factors, or by both. But we don't need definitive answers to such questions in order to take seriously the testimony of people like Kristi: The traditional path of heterosexual love and marriage is simply not available to them, try as they might to choose to be something other than what they are. As I write this, the national news has recently reported a decision by the leadership of Exodus International, a well-known "ex-gay" organization, to give up on all its ministries aimed at "curing" gay and lesbian people of their same-sex attraction.[4] The leadership of this group has finally concluded, after years of trying, that peoples' sexual orientation can't be changed and that telling them otherwise is a source of grievous psychological and spiritual harm. Even the highly traditional Roman Catholic Church has acknowledged in its official teaching that same-sex orientation is not a condition that people can either choose or reject for themselves.[5]

It was also clear from all the stories of brokenness I was encountering that Kristi and many others were not able to embrace a lifelong commitment to celibacy without crippling spiritual and psychological consequences. It is not immediately obvious why this should be the case. I remember sharing Kristi's story at a conference where I was speaking one time, only to be approached afterward by a very indignant member of the audience. "I am a single person," she said. "I have been striving very hard my whole life to live faithfully according to biblical sexual morality, and it's not always easy. How is it you can talk about the crippling, impossible burdens of celibate life for gay and lesbian people, but not for single men and women? Isn't that a double standard?"

In fact it's not a double standard, because traditional church teaching imposes requirements on gay and lesbian people that are far more drastic and far-reaching than anything it asks of single people. Yes, traditional church teaching counsels gay and single people alike to refrain from irresponsible sexual activity that is not coupled with covenant promises joining one's life together with one's partner. We will have much more to say on why this requirement makes sense in chapter 8. But for people like Kristi, the traditional teaching goes far beyond this.

Traditional teaching says to someone like Kristi that she must not only avoid irresponsible use of her sexuality while she is a single person but also forever give up hope of falling in love, getting married, and building a shared life with a person she loves. There is nothing comparable to this in the advice the church gives to single people, in fact it encourages them to find that special person they can share their life with. It is the traditional teaching's additional demand of gay people, that they must forever renounce even the hope and possibility of ever sharing in the kind of loving intimacy that is God's will for a good marriage, that makes the traditional teaching so spiritually and psychologically toxic for people like Kristi.

People sometimes fail to recognize this additional, heavy burden placed on gay people because they mistakenly believe that sex is the only issue on the table. I remember having a conversation one time with an older colleague who is usually quite wise and sensible. But on this particular occasion he said to me, "I just don't see how the church can say everyone has a *right* to have sex. That has never been the church's teaching." Indeed it has not. And if we put blinders on and pretend the issue is about only whether or not certain people should have sex, then it becomes very hard to register the difference between the church's traditional advice to single people and to gay people. In both cases it is advising a particular group to refrain from being sexually active. Church teaching has been communicating this message to single people for centuries. So why all the fuss when it comes to gay people?

What my colleague failed to appreciate is that for people like Kristi, the issue at stake isn't some right to be sexually active, but whether they can have love in their lives. Lots of people go without sex for various reasons, some for extended periods of time, without any sign of spiritual devastation or despair. But to ask someone to give up on the hope and possibility of ever getting to experience love and marriage—that is a far more serious matter.

In fact, in recognizing the overwhelming difficulty of a lifelong celibacy requirement, we stand squarely in line with traditional Protestant teaching about love and marriage. Starting in the early 1500s, leaders of the Protestant Reformation like Martin Luther and John Calvin vehemently criticized the Roman Catholic Church for imposing vows of lifelong celibacy on whole classes of people, as it was doing for monks, nuns, and priests.[6] These devout church Reformers argued that such vows were cruel. They required people to make sacrifices for God that were not in their power to make, resulting in widespread suffering, hypocrisy, and spiritual damage.[7] They also argued that celibacy requirements were unbiblical. Martin Luther emphasized that God created people for lifelong companionship with a spouse according to Genesis 2:18.[8] Both Jesus and Paul teach that celibacy is a gift given to only a few individuals. It is not an ability that God makes available to everyone (Matt. 9:16–17, 1 Cor. 7:7). John Calvin argued that it is an ungodly cruelty to impose a celibacy requirement indiscriminately on groups of people, the vast majority of whom have no gift or ability for it. Such an action substitutes spiritually damaging human regulations for the gracious gift God has provided in the institution of marriage.[9] And to those who claim that praying to God will help people find the strength to conform to such requirements, Calvin replies that God helps only those who walk in God's calling. People who despise the gift of marriage and try to embrace a celibacy for which they lack the requisite gifts are setting themselves against God and God's calling.[10]

Reviewing this Reformation teaching, I realized that there was nothing exaggerated, surprising, or unusual about the spiritual and psychological damage Kristi and other faithful gay people had experienced in trying to follow the church's traditional teaching. Protestant Christians had been arguing for centuries, on the basis of both Scripture and common experience, that requiring people to embrace a lifetime discipline of celibacy was cruel and damaging in the vast majority of cases.

What Kind of God?

These observations set the stage for some serious questions about God. What kind of God were we dealing with, I wondered, if the traditional condemnations of homosexuality were faithful and accurate reflections of the divine will? That would mean that God places Kristi and others like her in a situation from which there is no escape. They have absolutely no ability to wish or pray or choose their way out of their same-sex attraction, yet God condemns them unless they can change it. God further adds to the difficulty of the situation by withholding the gifts and calling that would make lifelong celibacy a realistic possibility.

If the traditional condemnations were true, then God had put Kristi and countless thousands like her in a position where she had exactly two options open to her: either she could embrace a life of celibacy for which she had no calling and experience all the brokenness, loss of faith, and alienation from God that I had seen following from that; or she could follow the path that led to love and personal fulfillment and stand condemned by God.

The more I thought about this picture, the more uncomfortable I felt with it. What kind of God would put people, through no fault of their own, in a situation where the only spiritual options available to them were broken alienation from God or divine condemnation? It was quite literally a situation of "damned if you do and damned if you don't." Kristi certainly had no say in whether she was gay or not. She had no ability to choose not to be gay. Try as she might, she was unable to manufacture a gift of celibacy for herself where none existed. The only way out for her was through seeking love and fulfillment within the bounds allotted her by her same-gender orientation. But if God truly condemned that path, then what? Then God had created Kristi simply as an object of condemnation, with no path available to her that led toward spiritual growth and wholeness, and no possibility of ever finding a life-giving relationship with God.

That was a distressing picture to contemplate, but fortunately I realized it was a picture that stood in utter contradiction to the portrait of God painted by Scripture. If the Bible and Christian proclamation are true and if Jesus really is God-with-us, then the clearest picture we have of what God is really like is Jesus himself. And there was absolutely nothing in Jesus' life or ministry that even remotely resembled the kind of gratuitous cruelty that would bring someone into existence only for the purpose of breaking or condemning them. To the contrary: Jesus' love and compassion broke through all the traditional barriers of his age, reaching out to embrace even his own enemies (Luke 23:34). Jesus spoke about God's heart rejoicing when the wandering find their way home (Luke 15) and about God's desire that no one be lost (Matt. 18:14). None of this fit with the picture of a God who would cruelly leave no path to grace for people like Kristi.

This picture, of a God who leaves gay people no option but condemnation, collided so dramatically with the witness of Scripture, I knew something had to be wrong with it. But what? I couldn't pretend that Kristi had the ability to stop being gay—if that were the case she would have left it behind a long time ago. I also couldn't deny the spiritual brokenness I had seen in her and dozens of others as the result of trying to embrace a life of celibacy for which they had no calling. The only part of the picture that was open to doubt was the traditional teaching condemning homosexuality. If this teaching were true, then the New Testament portrait of a loving and compassionate God was demonstrably false in the case of gay people like Kristi. Rather than go this route, I chose to stick with the Bible's testimony about God. The traditional condemnations of homosexuality had to be mistaken.

Summing Up

My encounters with Kristi and others like her brought to light two striking contradictions between the traditional church condemnations of homosexuality and the testimony of the Bible. First, the spiritual fruit I saw coming to the fore in lives of devout gay people who were trying to follow the traditional teaching was the exact opposite of what the Bible says will be the results of conforming our lives to the will of God. Instead of love, peace, joy, and closeness to God I was seeing bitterness, brokenness, and spiritual alienation. It was only when Kristi and others *gave up* trying to follow the traditional teaching that I saw the spiritual fruits emerging that would normally be associated with obedience to God's will.

Second, when I viewed the traditional teaching alongside the actual lived experience of people like Kristi, the result was a picture of an arbitrary and cruel God who closed off all possible avenues of escape for gay people and left them having to choose between psychological and spiritual brokenness on the one hand, and divine condemnation on the other. This picture differed strikingly from the portrait of a loving and compassionate God that is painted by the New Testament.

The combined weight of all this evidence forced me to conclude that the traditional condemnations were wrong. This recognition marked only the start of my journey, however. I had always assumed the traditional teaching was grounded in a straightforward manner on the testimony of Scripture. How could a teaching be in error if it was based on the Bible? I realized I would not be able to invest any confidence in my conclusions until I figured out how and why the traditional teaching had gone astray.

CHAPTER 2

◌◌◌

JESUS AND THE LAW

How Biblical Fragments Can Lead Us Astray

The new student was nothing if not enthusiastic. Before coming to seminary, Joe (not his real name) had been a successful high school football coach. I smiled as I saw him bringing to his ministerial studies the same can-do, hundred-and-ten-percent attitude that had served him so well on the gridiron and in the locker room. His commitment was inspiring.

Joe was feeling extra fired up after his first semester of seminary studies, and while he was home on Christmas break, he decided he would get some practice witnessing for his faith. As it happened, Joe's home was located not too far from a twenty-acre compound that served as the national headquarters of the Aryan Nations, a notorious white-supremacist hate group. What group of people could possibly stand more in need of the healing, reconciling love of Jesus Christ, Joe wondered. After praying and meditating about it for a time, Joe decided that God was calling him to bring the gospel to this group of heavily armed neo-Nazis.

Joe could be very persuasive when he needed to be. He managed to talk his way past the armed guard at the entrance to the compound and eventually found himself sitting face-to-face with Richard Butler, the national leader of the Aryan Nations. The conversation in Butler's office was cordial, with the white-supremacist leader asking Joe what he was there for. Joe took a deep breath and responded that he was there to tell him about the love of Jesus Christ. Opening his Bible, he started reading and explaining a number of Bible passages he had chosen for the occasion, beginning with John 3:16.

Recounting the story to me afterward, Joe said that Richard Butler listened politely to his witness. And when Joe was done, the older man reached into the drawer of his desk and brought out his own Bible. Opening it up, he began reading selected passages and explaining to Joe how these verses clearly showed the Bible to be the history of God's favored blessing bestowed upon the white race. Butler countered Joe's witness verse for verse and passage for passage with his own racist distortion of the Bible's message. Sad to say, there was no mass conversion to the gospel of love that day among the ranks of the neo-Nazis!

***

J oe's story helped me understand with a new clarity that even though certain ideas or teachings might have Bible verses to back them up, they could still be very far removed from the will of God. In particular this seemed to be a weakness of what I will call the "fragment method" of Bible interpretation. What Richard Butler and his followers did with the Bible was to identify a group of isolated, individual passages that they interpreted out of context and applied to their pet issue of race relations. Citing these fragments as a group, without any consideration of the broader witness of Scripture, they came to some disastrously false and mistaken conclusions about the message of the Bible and God's will for humankind.

A History of Bad Results

Joe's conversation with Richard Butler provided a vivid illustration of the dangers of the fragment method, but I soon realized that this problem was not limited to fringe groups standing outside the bounds of the mainstream church. The predecessor denominations of my own Presbyterian Church (U.S.A.) split over the issue of slavery in the mid 1800s. Going back and reading about that history, one discovers that the pro-slavery churches were defending their positions by appeal to the Bible! Isolated fragments, pulled out and interpreted apart from the overall witness of the Scripture, led those devout southern Presbyterians to conclude that their pro-slavery cause was blessed by God. Another such episode, which extends into more recent times, saw well-intentioned Christians appealing to isolated scriptural fragments as they argued to keep women in subordinate roles within both church and society.[1] The fragment method clearly has a long and sad history of providing "biblical" justification for teachings that we can recognize in hindsight as contrary to the will of God.

Would faithful Christians one day look back at the traditional condemnations of homosexuality and similarly shake their heads at us? I wondered. Witnessing the devastating fruits of that traditional teaching as it worked itself out in the lives of real human beings had given me some very strong reasons for believing it did *not* reflect the will of God. Could this be another case of the fragment method yielding false results?

Most of the biblical arguments I encountered that sought to justify and defend the traditional teaching seemed to employ this method. They lifted out from the Scripture seven fragments that seemed to reference some type of same-gender sexual behavior.[2] Some of these passages do not focus on sexual behavior as the main point of their teaching, mentioning it only as an illustration in the context of other discussions. But while a number of these passages refer to same-gender behaviors only in passing, all of them cast such behaviors in a negative light.

I started to wonder if the traditional teaching was paying sufficient attention to the broader witness of Scripture. These were seven isolated references, pulled from the Bible without much consideration of their surrounding contexts or the witness of Scripture as a whole. All of them spoke negatively about same-sex behaviors. (The particular behaviors these texts refer to will be important for us to consider down the road.) And the witness of these isolated passages was being used to justify the sweeping conclusion that God judges and condemns homosexual activity in all its forms, in all times and circumstances, without reservation or qualification. It seemed to be a classic example of the fragment method at work.

But was the recognition of this method sufficient to explain how a supposedly biblical teaching could turn out to be counter to the will of God? Maybe I was being too hard on the fragment method. After all, Christian believers appeal to isolated verses from Scripture all the time in support of faithful beliefs and practices. Was I stacking the deck against the method unfairly by shining the spotlight on unfortunate historical episodes like slavery and the oppression of women, while overlooking all the good results that this method produces daily in the lives of faithful Christians? In fact, there is a much stronger case to be made against the fragment method, and that case comes not from historical examples but from the pages of the New Testament!

The New Testament Critique of Biblical Law

I remember a prayer once offered by a dedicated leader of the Sunday school program in a church I was attending. "Thank you God," he said, "for giving us the Bible to teach us your rules for how we should live." Faithful people have always been inclined to read the Bible primarily as a book of rules, and with good reason. Lists of divinely authorized *thou shalts* and *thou shalt nots* figure very prominently in the text of Scripture. Loving God and wanting to obey and serve God have a way of going together, and so from Old Testament times down to the present day faithful people have pored over the text of Scripture, seeking to extract from it God's laws for how we are to live faithfully. We can see this exercise depicted in the pages of the New Testament itself, for example when the Pharisees test Jesus by asking him which of all the commands in the Old Testament Scripture he sees as most important (Matt. 22:34–39; see also Mark 12:28–34 and Luke 10:25–28).

But the New Testament is also shot through with the recognition that people who faithfully and conscientiously strive to follow all the rules—the Law of God—can still wind up straying very far afield from God's will and intention. People sometimes suffer from a kind of tunnel vision in how they interpret biblical Law, which causes them to miss its true purpose and significance. And at the end of the day, biblical rules and biblical Law do not have the power to refashion hearts in ways that are required for us to be truly faithful.

The New Testament records some very dramatic instances of people trying valiantly to follow biblical Law and still failing utterly to align their lives with God's will. Perhaps the most dramatic example is the Jewish leaders in Jerusalem, the "scribes and Pharisees," who failed to recognize Jesus as the Messiah. Many of these were devout and sincere people who were extremely serious about understanding and following the Law of God. And it was precisely this seriousness about following scriptural rules that tripped them up when they saw Jesus violating the Law as they understood it. Jesus did things contrary to their interpretation of the Law, like ignoring the prescribed ritual washings before eating and healing people on the Sabbath (Mark 7:1–5; John 9:1–41). As a result, many of these religious authorities decided that a rule breaker like Jesus couldn't possibly be the Messiah or the Son of God. Ultimately, these conclusions led them to support his crucifixion. It would be hard to imagine anything more opposed to God's loving will for human beings than handing God's incarnate Son over to the authorities for execution! And yet it wasn't godlessness, but their devotion to biblical Law as they understood it, that led many of these religious authorities to oppose Jesus.

A second striking instance of the Law's failure to align someone with the will of God comes from the personal experience of
the apostle Paul. Paul, by his own admission, was a zealous fol-
lower of biblical Law, and his devotion to it led him to oppose
and persecute the church (Gal. 1:13–14; Phil. 3:4–6; see also Acts
22:3–5). His rule following failed so completely to align him with
God's will that he referred to himself as "the least of the apostles,
unfit to be called an apostle because I persecuted the church of
God" (1 Cor. 15:9). Paul was acutely aware that it was only the
direct intervention of God that had saved him from the disastrous
course into which his devotion to the Law had led him: The risen
Christ had appeared to him on the road to Damascus and set his
life on a new course (Gal. 1:15–16; Acts 9:2–22).

In his letter to the Christians in Rome, Paul presents a striking meditation on the powerlessness of the written Law to lead
people into the life that God desires for them (Rom. 7:5 — 8:8),
even going so far as to call it the "the law of sin and death" (8:2).
Paul is clear, of course, that there is nothing bad or wrong about
the biblical commandments in themselves. The problem is that
human beings are blinded and deceived by sin to such a degree
that no written code, including the biblical commandments, has
the power to steer them toward true life in God (7:7–13).

Paul's own life required outside intervention from God to
open his eyes to the errors into which his devotion to the written Law had led him. In just the same way, Paul suggests that
it is the Holy Spirit working in the hearts of believers that will
overcome the limitations of the written code and lead them into
the life that God desires for them:

> For the law of the Spirit of life in Christ Jesus has set you free
> from the law of sin and of death. For God has done what the
> law, weakened by the flesh, could not do.
>
> (8:2–3)

In his old life as a Pharisee, Paul had tried desperately to faithfully
obey and follow God's will using the written commands of Scripture as his guide. But contrary to all his hopes and expectations,

Paul found himself unwittingly opposing God's work as he persecuted the newly formed church. As conscientious as Paul was, his devotion to the written rules contained in the Scripture proved insufficient to align him with the will of God. Paul required something extra to set him on the path of faithfulness.

In Paul's case that "something extra" was a post-resurrection appearance of Jesus that opened his eyes to the work of God taking place in and through the life of the church. This need to look up from the written code and see what God was actually doing is also reflected in advice that Jesus gave to John the Baptist about keeping aligned with God's work in the world. The Gospel of Luke records an episode in which John dispatches messengers from his prison cell to seek out Jesus and ask him, "Are you the one who is to come, or are we to wait for another?" (Luke 7:20). Perhaps John, like the scribes and Pharisees, was starting to get rattled by all the ways in which Jesus' actions placed him at odds with traditional understandings of what obedience to the written commands should look like.

Jesus' reply to John was essentially to open his eyes to the work of God taking place in and through his ministry: "Go and tell John what you have seen and heard: the blind receive their sight, the lame walk, the lepers are cleansed, the deaf hear, the dead are raised, the poor have good news brought to them" (7:22). For John the Baptist, as for Paul, the errors and confusion that arose from attending only to the written commands of Scripture found correction when Jesus helped him see and understand what was actually taking place in the world around him.

Reflecting on this pattern, I realized that it was similar to what I had been experiencing. Perhaps I was on more solid ground than I thought when I allowed observations of what was actually happening in the lives of believing gay people to raise questions about the traditional condemnations of homosexuality that were based entirely on fragments of the written, biblical Law! Was it possible that the Holy Spirit would correct peoples' misunderstanding of the Bible surrounding this issue, in the same way as had happened with the "biblical" cases supporting slavery and the oppression of women?

The Journey So Far . . .

At the beginning of this journey, described in chapter 1, I had found strong reasons for doubting whether the church's traditional condemnations of homosexuality were in line with the will of God. Now I found myself considering how it was possible for those teachings to be mistaken, even though they seemed to be based on a reasonably straightforward reading of individual passages taken from the Bible.

I found strong evidence, both in the history of the church and in the testimony of the New Testament, supporting the conclusion that this fragment approach to interpreting biblical Law is unreliable and highly prone to error. These findings lent further credibility to my initial strong suspicions that the traditional condemnations were contrary to the will and plan of God.

In concluding that the traditional teachings were mistaken, however, I realized that my journey with the Bible was only beginning. When God helped Paul and other early followers of Jesus to jettison their false and misleading understandings of biblical Law, the result was to correct their understanding of the Scripture, not throw it out altogether. Jesus did not come to abolish the Law (Matt. 5:17).

Instead, God worked through the risen Christ and the Holy Spirit to help the early church come to a newer and truer understanding of the Scriptures. Luke records a picture of this process taking place as he relates the encounter between the risen Christ and two of his disciples on the road to Emmaus: "Then beginning with Moses and all the prophets, [Jesus] interpreted to them the things about himself in all the Scriptures" (Luke 24:27).

Erroneous readings of biblical Law led many people to reject Jesus. When those errors came to light, Christ led the church toward better and more faithful ways of interpreting the Bible. These new interpretations made it clear that the Law and the Prophets had been pointing to Jesus from the very beginning.

As I attempted to apply this to my own situation, I realized it was not enough simply to recognize that traditional condemnations of homosexuality were mistaken. Such a recognition wouldn't carry much credibility unless it was accompanied by a truer, better reading of the Bible that showed in a positive way how gay people were recipients of God's blessing. It was to the task of developing that truer, better reading that I now had to turn.

CHAPTER 3

∞∞∞

WITH ALL YOUR MIND

Reading the Bible Faithfully and Responsibly

The year was AD 177, and the church in Lyons, France, was in crisis.[1] Beloved Pothinus, the very first Christian bishop of the city, had been mercilessly slaughtered in a persecution carried out by the Roman authorities. In the aftermath of the massacre, the church turned to a faithful priest named Irenaeus to assume the dangerous task of leading the local flock.

Irenaeus was determined to be a faithful guide and defender of the congregations entrusted to his care. He soon discovered that the threats facing the church were internal as well as external. A rival system of religious teaching, called Valentinian Gnosticism, was sowing great confusion among Christian believers in Lyons and elsewhere. Irenaeus knew that this body of esoteric ideas bore little resemblance to the teaching of Christ and his apostles. The good bishop was fully confident in this judgment because his own education in the faith had been only one generation of teachers removed from Jesus' disciples. As a young man, Irenaeus had heard first-hand the Christian teaching of Bishop Polycarp of Smyrna, who in turn had received instruction from Jesus' own disciple John, the son of Zebedee.[2]

Especially confusing for the faithful of Irenaeus's time was the way the Valentinians supported their teaching with quoted snippets of Scripture. Irenaeus realized that these false teachers were lifting out isolated fragments of Scripture without any regard for their original order or context. Describing the Valentinians' use of the Bible, Irenaeus invited his flock to imagine a skilled artist who had arranged many precious, colored stones into a beautiful mosaic portrait of a king. Now consider, said Irenaeus, if someone were to take the mosaic completely apart, and then reassemble all the original colored stones into a brand-new picture. Except this time the arrangement of stones was such that instead of the beautiful portrait of the king, they now depict a crudely crafted image of a dog. And suppose further, said Irenaeus, that this person then went around showing off the reassembled dog portrait and saying to everyone who saw it, "Behold, the king!" Irenaeus pointed out that even though every single stone in this work came from the original mosaic of the king, it was no longer a picture of the king in any meaningful sense.

This, said Irenaeus, is what the Valentinians do with Scripture. Every single passage they cite is true and authentic Scripture. But the Gnostic teachers have lifted these scriptural fragments out of context and rearranged them in such a way that they no longer convey a true portrait of the One to whom the original Scriptures bear witness.[3]

Irenaeus's description of the rearranged mosaic helped me understand more clearly what was wrong with the fragment method of Scripture interpretation. Isolated passages of Scripture can be lifted out and combined to provide support for all sorts of odd ideas, from slavery to white supremacy to the subordination of women to the blanket condemnation of gay and lesbian relationships. If a person pays no attention to the original biblical portrait of God's redeeming love in Christ, the colored stones of the original scriptural mosaic can be rearranged to depict and justify almost anything. The fragment method is unreliable because it pieces together isolated passages without any regard for the "big picture" of the Bible's overall witness.

Having recognized the drawbacks of the fragment method in providing guidance for questions surrounding gay and lesbian relationships, I was looking for a better way of interpreting and understanding the Scripture, one that would be a more reliable guide to God's will for the church. As I reflected on Irenaeus's mosaic analogy, I realized that a more reliable and faithful interpretation would be one that takes steps to maintain connection with the "big picture" of the Bible's witness—the original portrait of the king. Such an interpretation would need to be in touch with the central themes and larger concerns of the Bible's message, while also respecting the integrity and particular witness of relevant individual passages.

As a Presbyterian Christian, I was fortunate to find myself standing within a long tradition of careful biblical interpretation that was concerned to do exactly this. Though its practice has sometimes fallen short, my church over the centuries has developed a number of important guidelines for interpreting the Bible thoughtfully and well.[4] These rules of thumb do not provide an infallible recipe for faithful church teaching, but they do provide concrete tools for keeping our interpretations in touch with the central themes and overarching concerns of the Bible's witness.

Principle One:
Coherent, Good Sense

The first rule I determined to keep in mind as I set out to reexamine the Bible's witness on sexuality was the conviction that faithful interpretations of the Bible should make coherent, good sense. It is true that Scripture occasionally presents situations in which particular commands of God do not seem reasonable in the moment they are received. God's command for Abraham to sacrifice his only son, Isaac (Gen. 22:1–19), and Jesus' teaching about nonresistance to evil and turning the other cheek (Matt. 5:39) both have the appearance of leading to harmful results. But in the broader context of the Bible's witness—God's sparing of Isaac at the end of the Genesis account and God's vindication of Jesus' nonresistance in the resurrection—we see how the underlying sense of such episodes shines through.[5]

The reasons for God's commands should be understandable. This sounds simple, but it is so far-reaching and so contrary to ways we often think about the Bible that it is worth considering carefully.

I started to grasp the importance of this "good-sense principle" when I considered what Christian discipleship would be like if we had no reason for expecting that God's commands would make sense to us. What would be the effect on the life of faith if God had simply scattered arbitrary commandments across the landscape of our lives?

Such commands would not have any discernible rhyme or reason to them, and obeying them would not appear to serve any useful purpose apart from testing our obedience and demonstrating our respect for God's authority.[6] Indeed if obedience to these commands produced harmful or nonsensical results, they would simply be a greater test of our faith.

I am using exaggerated descriptions of this "arbitrary rules" approach to biblical Law, and at first hearing it probably sounds a bit outlandish. But as we saw in chapter 1, many defenders of the traditional condemnations of homosexuality, knowingly or not, accept quite harmful outcomes for their gay and lesbian neighbors for the sake of fidelity to a particular interpretation of biblical rules. It seems that a great many of us are accustomed to thinking about biblical teaching in terms of arbitrary rules, especially when the topic is sex.

These patterns of thinking find illustration in a recent essay by Tim Challies, a pastor who describes the single-minded focus in many evangelical congregations on the rule that young people should be virgins when they get married.[7] This single-minded focus on virginity, writes Challies, yields situations like the pre-marriage course where the young man who burned up his teens and early twenties staring at tens of thousands of pornographic images somehow thinks he holds the moral high ground over the young woman who had sex one time with one boyfriend. After all, he is a virgin and she is not.[8]

Treating virginity as an arbitrary rule also produces Christian teens who engage in a wide variety of sexual behaviors that bypass or stop short of conventional sexual intercourse. Challies observes that these young people assume such activities are less freighted with moral significance because, technically speaking, they do not compromise a person's virginity.

Treating biblical sexual regulations as arbitrary expressions of divine authority also imbues them with a kind of radioactive aura that can do enormous spiritual damage to those who, even once, yield to temptation and fall short. Devout young people finding themselves in such situations, writes Challies, "may feel they have sinned irreversibly, that this was the greatest of all sins, that they have been relegated to a lesser class of Christian, that they can only ever disappoint that future spouse."[9]

The point here is not that saving oneself for marriage is a bad thing or that sexual regulations in general are outmoded. The point is that if we treat even the noblest moral teaching as an arbitrary rule and fail to consider the reasons and purposes that underlie it, our attempts at obedience will likely produce distorted and damaging results. Any adequate interpretation of the Bible's moral teaching will include not just rules or principles for guiding behavior, but an *understanding of the reasons* why such principles make sense.

Arbitrary Rules and Slippery Slopes

A strong indicator that such reasons have *not* been a prominent feature of the church's traditional condemnations of homosexuality is the prevalence of slippery-slope arguments in defense of the traditional teaching. In discussions about these issues, I have often heard arguments that go something like this: If the church gives ground on homosexuality and says it is OK for gay people to get married, then the church will have no right to object to other terrible sexual behaviors like polygamy, bestiality, and sex with underage minors. These arguments assume that reconsidering any one aspect of the church's sexual teaching will catapult us headlong down a slippery slope, making it impossible for the church to uphold any standards for sexual behavior whatsoever. Such arguments are scary, and for that reason alone they sometimes have persuasive force.

But slippery-slope arguments work only if we view the church's sexual teaching as a set of arbitrary regulations, which we have no reason to follow apart from respect for the divine authority that put them in place. In a world of rules that have no underlying sense or reason, the slippery-slope argument makes some sense. An illustration helps clarify why this is the case:

When my children were young I often joined them playing with blocks. One of our favorite challenges was to see how tall a tower we could make by stacking blocks one on top of the other. The end result was usually a precariously balanced structure, the foundation of which was a single block resting on the tabletop. The structure of such a tower is similar to the structure of biblical Law that consists only of arbitrary rules. Just as our whole tower was supported by the tabletop at a single point, so the whole structure of biblical Law finds support in this case from a single principle, namely our human respect for the rules as we currently understand them. Having only one point of support makes for a very unstable structure: adjusting any single block in our tower was liable to bring the whole pile crashing down to the tabletop. Similarly, making adjustments in any one area of biblical teaching (like homosexuality) undermines the respect we have for established understandings of all the rules and brings the whole structure tumbling down. Slippery-slope arguments work when the *only* reason we can give for upholding biblical Law is our human respect for the rules as currently understood.

But the situation is very different if God issues particular commandments for good reasons that we have the ability to uncover and understand. This situation resembles a different game we used to play with blocks. In this game we would keep all the blocks on the tabletop, using them to outline a floor plan for a castle or fort or many-roomed mansion. In such a structure, adjusting any single block would have no effect on any of the other blocks, because each block was supported in its own place by the tabletop.

Similarly, if God's commands have a sensible purpose, then adjusting our understanding in one area of biblical Law will have absolutely no effect on other commandments, because each of these other regulations will continue to find support in the good and understandable reasons that uphold it. Setting foot on this slope is perfectly safe because the slope is not slippery! Rethinking same-gender relationships will pose absolutely no threat to the church's teaching about bestiality, for example, because all the good reasons for thinking bestiality a bad idea will still be in place. We will have much more to say about these reasons in subsequent chapters.

The fact that slippery-slope arguments continue to be widely used and cited in contemporary discussions of sexuality are a sign that a great many Christians think about the Bible's teaching in accordance with the arbitrary-rules theory. In this view, biblical commands are regulations upheld by divine authority alone, and seeking reasons or understandable purposes underlying them is beside the point: "God said it, I believe it, that settles it (even if I don't understand it!)."

The prevalence of this kind of thinking made me aware that putting forward a good-sense principle of scriptural interpretation would require a great many people to change the way they have been thinking about the Bible. What right did I or anyone else have to urge on them such a radical change in their thinking? Is it really faithful to God's authority to say that, if we are to have confidence that our interpretation is on the right track, we need to find good-sense reasons for the Bible's teaching?

Biblical Reasons for Seeking Sense
in the Commandments

In fact, the Bible itself gives us very strong reasons for hold-ing to the good-sense principle of Scripture interpretation. All through the Old Testament, the assumption is that following God's ways will cause people to flourish. This divinely given wisdom is more valuable than silver or gold or precious jewels, because those who understand it find life (Prov. 8:10–11, 35).

An analogy from earthly parenting is helpful in understanding this. When my three children were younger and living at home, my wife and I were very active in providing them with daily guid-ance and direction—some of it quite firm! We did not do this because we wanted to flaunt our authority over them or test their obedience. When we told them "Do this!" or "Don't do that!" it was because we loved them and wanted them to grow and flour-ish. "Don't stick your fingers in the electrical socket." "Do brush your teeth before you go to bed at night." Our children did not always fully comprehend, in the moment, why we made rules like these. But we told them these things because we dearly wanted them to be safe and healthy and happy. We were not perfect par-ents, as our children will quite rightly point out, but on our good days, at least, there were *reasons* behind the instruction we gave to them. We provided them guidance because we loved them deeply and wanted the very best for them.

So it is with God. Though there are times when God's com-mandments seem mysterious to us, God is not an arbitrary tyrant who makes capricious demands to test our devotion. God does not set up meaningless hoops for us to jump through. God has lovingly created and fashioned us in God's own image, and the *reason* God provides us guidance in the form of commandments and divine wisdom is because God loves us deeply and wants our lives to flourish. God gives us the commandments *for our good* (Deut. 10:13).

For this reason, we stand on solidly biblical foundations when we say that a good test of whether we have understood the Bible's teaching correctly is whether or not we can discern the loving *reasons* that stand behind it. This takes effort some-times, for we are sinful human beings prone to pride and self-deception. But putting forth our best efforts in community with one another and praying for God's help, we ought to be able to catch a glimpse of *how* God's guidance and wisdom will be good for us if we follow it. If we are not able to see that, it may be a sign that we have not understood God's guidance correctly.

I realized this was exactly the logic I had followed when I noted a recurring pattern in which devout gay and lesbian peo-ple who tried to follow traditional church teaching often wound up as broken people, alienated from God and the church. It did not look at all as if this supposedly biblical teaching was work-ing for their good, and that led me to question whether I had understood the Bible correctly on this issue.

Divine and Human Rationality

There are even deeper reasons given in the New Testament for expecting a correct understanding of God's will to make reason-able good sense. The writers of the New Testament encountered a reality almost beyond imagining in Jesus of Nazareth. As the writer of John's Gospel groped for words and concepts to express what he had experienced, he seized on a concept from the philosophy of his day to express what he was trying to say: Jesus is the Logos, said John (1:1–14).

This Greek term means that Christ is the *Word* of God, the divine wisdom and rationality that holds the entire cosmos in existence and keeps it working in orderly fashion:

> All things came into being through him, and without him not one thing came into being.
>
> (1:3)

> All things have been created through him and for him. He him-self is before all things, and in him all things hold together.
>
> (Col. 1:16b–17)

The Logos is the divine wisdom that undergirds what we would today call "the laws of nature." It is the rational pattern that determines how the world and human life function, how they are "wired." And in Jesus of Nazareth, we come face to face with this wisdom and rationality of God, present among us as a human being. This is the incredible claim of the New Testament writers. In Jesus, the divine Logos took on human flesh and came to dwell among us as one of us. Christ is God's wisdom and rationality personified.

We might think that God's wisdom and rationality would be far too high and exalted for frail human beings to grasp or even approach. But the New Testament declares otherwise. If the divine Logos could be fully present among us in the human person named Jesus, this means that human nature and divine rationality must be compatible. They are able to coexist in the same person.

Building on this insight, some of the early Greek theologians recognized and taught that human beings were *logikos*, rational creatures made in the image of the divine Logos (see Gen. 1:27). This means we can have confidence that human beings who are created in the image of the Logos will be capable of grasping and understanding certain aspects of God's own rationality. While finite creatures can never hope to completely comprehend God, women and men are rational creatures who have potential to grasp, at least in part, the contours of the divine wisdom, the Logos, that undergirds the cosmos.

This explains why human beings are capable of doing natural science. On the face of it, there is no reason to expect that human brains would be able to understand the natural laws that guide the orderly workings of the universe. Why do we not relate to the universe the way ants or other insects do, as something so vast and so totally beyond our abilities that we could never even begin to comprehend it? It is because human minds, fashioned in the image of the divine Logos, are able to understand, at least in part, the natural laws that the Logos has brought into being.

Similarly, our creation in the divine image gives us the capability to grasp and understand the *moral* structure of the cosmos.

The goal of the biblical commandments is to bring our lives into harmony with this moral structure that the divine Logos has brought into being. And our creation in the image of the Logos gives us confidence that we will be able, with effort, to grasp and understand some of the divine rationality—the divine reasons—that stand behind the commandments.

"You shall love the Lord your God with all your . . . mind!" This is not just a peripheral concern of the Scriptures. It is part of the two-verse summary of the Law that Jesus identifies as encapsulating the message of the entire Scripture (Mark 12:30; Matt. 22:37; Luke 10:27). It makes sense that this principle should be so important; God creates us as rational creatures in the image of the divine Logos. We are not dumb beasts responding reflexively to rote commands, like the dogs that Pavlov conditioned to salivate at the sound of a bell. We are rational moral agents created in the image and likeness of God. It would therefore be completely contrary to God's purposes for us if we refused to *think* about God's commandments. God deliberately creates us with the ability to penetrate beneath the surface of the Bible's teachings and seek the reasons—the rational good sense—that stands behind the divine commandments. Until we have achieved a grasp of the coherent good sense of God's commands, we cannot claim to have understood them as God intends.

Principle Two: Christ-Centered Interpretation

I was searching for ways to avoid the hazards of the fragment method and keep my understanding of the Bible's teaching about sexuality in touch with the "big picture" of the Bible's witness. Clearly the requirement that an interpretation of the Bible's teaching should make coherent good sense was going to be very important. But I also came across other classical guidelines for interpreting Scripture that had stood the test of time. One of the most significant of these was that any correct understanding of the Bible's teaching should be grounded and centered in Christ. Once again, this was no arbitrary principle cooked up out of some pious person's imagination. It had deep roots in the witness of Scripture itself.

The incarnation, life, death, and resurrection of Jesus constitutes the heart and center of the faith for Christians and, hence, of the Bible's witness. Jesus says at one point, "Whoever has seen me has seen the Father" (John 14:9). That means that in Jesus we have direct access to the God to whom the Old Testament bears witness. So if our goal is to keep a particular interpretation of the Bible's teaching grounded in the "big picture" of the scriptural witness, Jesus will necessarily be the central reference point for our understanding of the Bible's message.

Keeping Jesus at the center of our biblical interpretation also makes sense in light of the particular character of the incarnation. Historic Christian teaching makes clear that Jesus is not just fully God; he is also fully human. In Jesus we see the clearest, fullest example possible of what God intends human beings to be, women and men alike. So if the goal of biblical Law is to guide us toward becoming the people God intended us to be, it follows that the purpose of the Law from the very beginning was to help us become more like Jesus.

This means that if an interpretation of biblical Law fails to have Jesus as its central reference point, that is a sure sign that we have misunderstood the Bible's teaching. Christ is the focal point of God's intention for human beings, and so his life and ministry and example must figure prominently in any interpretation of the Bible's guidance for our lives.

Principle Three: Interpreting Scripture by Scripture

Yet another classic principle of Bible interpretation says that we should "interpret Scripture by Scripture." This principle helps us keep our understanding in tune with the big picture of the Bible's witness by interpreting individual passages with reference to the rest of Scripture. It also says that if a particular passage is giving us trouble, we should seek help with it from other, clearer parts of the biblical text.

I realized I had actually been following this principle when I concluded that there were problems with the traditional condemnations of homosexuality (see ch. 1). Following those condemnations seemed to contradict the broader witness of Scripture. Such action produced damaging consequences in people's lives that seemed the opposite of what the Bible said the fruits of faithfulness should look like. And the picture of God that emerged from the condemnations seemed significantly opposed to the New Testament's witness to God's love in Jesus. While Jesus called all people to himself, the traditional condemnations seemed to consign certain people to an inevitable shipwreck of their faith.

After noting these problems with the traditional interpretation of the fragments, I was now seeking an understanding of God's will for gay and lesbian people that was grounded more solidly in the "big picture" of scriptural testimony about the nature of God. In other words, I was seeking to interpret the witness of problem passages by recourse to the broader witness of the Bible. This is what it means to interpret Scripture by Scripture.

Principle Four: Interpreting Passages in Context

Yet another straightforward but very important guideline for correctly interpreting Scripture is seeking to understand particular passages in both their biblical and historical contexts. Proper understanding of a passage should take seriously its setting in the Bible. In a sense, this is just a variation of the "interpret Scripture by Scripture" principle.

Paying attention to context also means that we seek to learn as much as we can about the historical circumstances in which the passage was first written and heard so that we get a sense of what it would have meant to its original hearers. For example, consider certain Bible passages that refer to the institution of slavery without offering any criticism of it (see, e.g., Col. 4:1; Titus 2:9–10; 1 Pet. 2:18–20). If we view these words apart from their historical context, it might be possible to conclude, as some previous generations of slave-owning Christians unfortunately did, that human slavery is an acceptable institution in the eyes of God.

If, however, we take seriously the historical context of such passages, we will realize that these words were written to members of an ancient Greco-Roman society that was wholly dependent on slavery for its economic survival. The issue of abolishing slavery simply was not on the table in that historical context because nobody would have believed that such a reform was even possible. Knowing this helps us recognize that the absence of objections to the institution of slavery in such passages is a time-bound reflection of the human historical circumstances in which they were written and not a timeless reflection of God's will and intentions for human life. Historical context is important!

Principle Five: Understanding the Purpose of the Lawgiver

A final guideline for interpreting Scripture faithfully comes from the pen of John Calvin, a leader of the Protestant Reformation whom Presbyterians honor as one of the founders of their church. I was seeking an understanding of the Bible's teaching about human sexuality that would conform to the other guidelines and provide a more faithful understanding than was possible with the fragment method. Calvin helped me figure out where to start. As Calvin prepares to explain the meaning of the Ten Commandments for his readers, he states a very important principle. In order to rightly understand and interpret biblical Law, he says, we must understand the purpose of God that stands behind the commandment:

> Thus in each commandment we must investigate what it is concerned with; then we must seek out its purpose, until we find

what the Lawgiver testifies there to be pleasing or displeasing to himself.[10]

This is not some odd or specialized principle that is limited to the field of biblical interpretation. We run across it almost every day as people strive to understand one another: "Why did he say that?" "What is she trying to get at with that statement?" With questions like these, people are trying to understand the reasons people say the things they do.

When judges in our court system seek to interpret the meaning and proper application of a particular law, they will sometimes refer to the *legislative intent* that stands behind it: What was the underlying purpose of the law in the minds of the legislators who voted it into existence? What was the legislative body that adopted the law trying to accomplish? Making sure we grasp the purpose or intention that stands behind a particular statement or regulation is simply a commonsense means of ensuring that we have understood it properly.

As simple as it is, however, this principle provided powerful guidance as I sought to faithfully understand the Bible's teaching in matters of human sexuality. It suggested that my starting point should be to ask about the purposes of God that stand behind the Bible's teaching about love and marriage, bodies and sexuality. What was God's intention in making these gifts a part of human life? What was God trying to accomplish in giving women and men the capacity to experience one another in these ways? These questions gave me a starting point for trying to understand in a faithful and responsible way what the Bible's teaching on sexuality was all about.

CHAPTER 4

⌒

"THIS IS MY BODY,
GIVEN FOR YOU"

God's Plan for Love, Marriage, and Sexuality

⌒

I am having a casual conversation over coffee with a youth pastor. "The kids come to me with so many questions," she says. "They are always asking, 'Where should I draw the line with my boyfriend?' and 'What do I think about the things certain members of the group do on their cell phones and computers?' So many of the situations they bring up are not dealt with in Scripture directly. I don't want to be a prude with them, and I live in the real world. But I take the Bible seriously, and I want them to be decent Christians. How do I find my bearings in figuring out what to tell them?"

⌒

I was beginning to realize that a great many people, pastors included, were puzzling over how to draw relevant and faithful guidance about contemporary sexual issues from the pages of Scripture. Beyond the repetition of a few very traditional "Thou Shalt Nots," a lot of faithful people simply didn't know where to begin.

I saw that a faithful and truly biblical understanding of God's will for gay and lesbian people would need to be grounded in the "big picture" of the Bible's witness about marriage and sexuality. Focusing only on isolated scriptural fragments had led to disastrous results on many other issues in the past, and I didn't want to risk being similarly misled on this current question.

It was also becoming clear that a good way to get in touch with this big picture was to ask about the purpose of the Lawgiver: Looking at the grand sweep of the Bible's witness, what are the highest purposes that emerge for love, sex, and marriage? Why did God invent these gifts and make them a part of human life? What was God trying to accomplish in creating human beings with the capability of entering into these experiences? What purposes did God have in mind for our use and enjoyment of these gifts? I hoped that answering questions such as these would give me a framework for thinking faithfully about sexual issues generally, including questions about gay marriage. I set myself the task of surveying the biblical text in order to seek answers to these questions.

Sexuality and Spiritual Life

Early on in this process I found myself feeling uncomfortable. Speaking about God and sex in the same breath had a kind of irreligious feel about it, as if these topics didn't belong together in the same room. I think a great many people feel this way because we are accustomed to thinking of sexuality as something "low" and material and earthly. This earthly reality stands in distinct contrast to the higher, spiritual dimensions of life that are the concerns of the Bible and the Christian faith. Many of us assume that becoming a really spiritual person means we must rise above our concern with earthly, materials realities, and most especially the concerns of the body. Sex and spirituality just don't fit together well.

As I continued my study, however, I came to see that this tendency to place life in the body in opposition to spirituality and religious life actually runs counter to the message of Scripture. Our perceived opposition between bodies and spirits actually comes to us as an inheritance from ancient, non-Christian philosophy. Classical philosophers like Plato described spiritual enlightenment as a process in which the soul rises above the distracting concerns of the body and the material world in order to enter into communion with the pure spiritual essences of ultimate reality. Thousands of years later, this way of thinking lives on in many of us; it seems natural to think of religion as focusing exclusively on higher matters of the spirit, while earthly matters of the body and physical existence occupy a separate, much lower plane.

The Bible views bodily existence in a much more positive light, however. Far from placing spirituality and sexuality in opposition, God is the inventor of sex in the scriptural account. At the very beginning of the Bible—in Genesis chapters 1 and 2—we find God's creation of human beings in the divine image standing in the closest possible proximity to our creation as male and female:

> So God created humankind in his image,
>   in the image of God he created them;
>   male and female he created them.
> (Gen. 1:27)

This passage suggests that there is no opposition between our creation in the image of God and our creation as sexual beings, male and female. God creates human beings not as disembodied spiritual essences but as flesh-and-blood, physical creatures. We are bodies and spirits both.

Coming right on the heels of this affirmation of our nature as sexual beings, Genesis 2 lifts up the gift of marriage as an important part of God's good creation. The creation account in Genesis 1 depicts God speaking into existence all the different parts of creation—the sea and the dry land, the plants and the stars overhead, the various kinds of animals, and finally human beings. And after each particular act of creation, Genesis emphasizes the wonderful blessing that God's work represents: "And God saw that it was good" (vv. 4, 10, 12, 18, 21, 25, 31). But in the second part of the creation story in the following chapter, there is one aspect of God's handiwork that does not reflect this original, primeval goodness. In one of the most gracious verses in all of Scripture, God declares, "It is not good that the man should be alone; I will make him a helper as his partner" (2:18).

Human beings, in the Bible's account, are created by God for intimate communion with a partner. Adam's joyous cry of recognition as God introduces Eve to him reflects his liberation from the primal solitude that was the single defective component of the original creation.

It is noteworthy that Adam's passionate joy comes in response to his recognition that Eve shares the same physical nature with him, bones and flesh. Human beings are created for deep communion with a partner, and because we are creatures possessing both bodies and spirits, this communion is all-encompassing; it involves our physical, bodily natures as well as our emotional and spiritual capacities. Genesis 2 immediately lifts up marriage as the social arrangement toward which this God-given need for communion draws us: "Therefore a man leaves his father and his mother and clings to his wife, and they become one flesh" (v. 24). Lest there be any doubt that this clinging together includes a bodily, sexual communion along with spiritual and emotional union, the very next verse adds: "And the man and his wife were both naked, and were not ashamed."

The message of Genesis 1 and 2 is unmistakable: Physical bodies and sexuality are the good gifts of God. God has graciously created us with the need and capacity for intimate fellowship with another human being. Within that fellowship, bodies, no less than spirits and emotions, are the chosen instruments God has provided; both bodies and spirits are involved in helping us overcome our solitude and grow into deep, encompassing communion with a beloved partner.

A Surprising Turn

The Genesis texts are far from the last word the Bible offers on love, marriage, and sexuality. As the scriptural witness unfolds, a striking new pattern emerges; the biblical writers begin to employ the language of love and marriage to describe not only the connection of human beings to each other but also the connection between human beings and God.

The Song of Solomon occupies a middle ground between everyday understandings of love and marriage and the use of marital language in depicting God's connection to human beings. On its surface, this book is a sensual and beautiful love poem celebrating the passion that binds two lovers together. It would be hard to imagine a more ringing affirmation of the goodness of love and sexuality in God's eyes. But beyond its surface level, traditional interpretations of the Song of Solomon have viewed it as an image of the love that binds God and Israel to each other. Later Christian interpretation carried this theme forward, treating it as a symbolic description of the passionate love that binds Christ to the church or to the individual soul.

The Bible's use of marital language to describe the connection of God with God's people becomes much more explicit in the prophets. Isaiah, Jeremiah, and Hosea all speak of God as being "married" to the chosen people of Israel: "For your Maker is your husband, / the LORD of hosts is his name" (Isa. 54:5; see also Jer. 2:2):

> [Y]ou shall be called My Delight Is in Her,
> and your land Married;
> for the LORD delights in you
> and your land shall be married.
> For as a young man marries a young woman,
> so shall your builder marry you,
> and as the bridegroom rejoices over the bride,
> so shall your God rejoice over you.
> (Isa. 62:4b–5)

On that day, says the LORD, you will call me, "My husband,"
. . . And I will take you for my wife forever; I will take you for
my wife in righteousness and in justice, in steadfast love, and in
mercy. I will take you for my wife in faithfulness; and you shall
know the LORD.

(Hos. 2:16,19–20)

This is a striking and unusual concept, to think that the Lord
and Creator of the whole universe would be "married" to human
beings! If it didn't occur in the pages of Scripture, we might
think it almost blasphemous!

The tone of these references is not always positive. Jeremiah
and Hosea both continue speaking of God's marriage to Israel,
but they extend the description to speak of Israel's unfaithfulness as divorce from God or as adultery:

[People] saw that for all the adulteries of that faithless one, Israel,
I had sent her away with a decree of divorce; yet her false sister
Judah did not fear, but she too went and played the whore. . . .
 As a faithless wife
 leaves her husband,
 so you have been faithless
 to me, O house of Israel,
 says the LORD.
(Jer. 3:8, 20)

When the LORD first spoke through Hosea, the LORD said to
Hosea, "Go, take for yourself a wife of whoredom and have
children of whoredom, for the land commits great whoredom
by forsaking the LORD."

(Hos. 1:2)

These Old Testament descriptions of the marriage bond that
connects God with God's people carry over into the New Testament as well. In fact, the New Testament writers infuse the
image with new life and fresh reality as the marriage language
reaches out to incorporate Jesus' relationship with his followers.

In John's Gospel, John the Baptist describes the beginnings of Jesus' earthly ministry as a bridegroom arriving at his wedding celebration (3:29), and the very first of the miraculous signs pointing to Jesus' identity takes place in the context of a wedding banquet (2:1–11). Jesus himself compares his presence among his disciples to a bridegroom's presence at a wedding feast (Matt. 9:14–15; Luke 5:33–35), and he uses images of a wedding banquet to describe the future consummation of God's kingdom on earth (Matt. 22:1–14; 25:1–13; Luke 12:35–38). The book of Revelation echoes and amplifies this theme from the Gospels, describing Jesus' second coming as the marriage of Christ the bridegroom to his bride, the church (Rev. 19:7–9; 21:2, 9; 22:17). And Paul speaks of his missionary work as an effort to prepare a fitting bride for Christ: "I feel a divine jealousy for you, for I promised you in marriage to one husband, to present you as a chaste virgin to Christ" (2 Cor. 11:2).

These recurring images, describing God's relation to us as a marriage or Christ as the husband of the church, seem striking, almost to the point of being shocking. Yet the number of times they occur throughout the Bible suggests they are very important to the Bible's overall witness. What are we to make of them?

The Divine Reality
behind the Marriage References

At first I thought such passages were putting forward a simple comparison: God's love for us is *like* the love that binds a husband and wife together in a good marriage. But I soon realized that the comparison runs in the other direction: the love that binds people together in marriage is *like* the love that exists in the heart of God. And this likeness is not simply a surface similarity; it is part and parcel of the divine image in human beings. The biblical writers can describe God's love for us as marital love, because human marital love is itself an image of the love that has existed from all eternity in the heart of God.

To speak of God's love for human beings as marital love is therefore a direct application of the teaching of Genesis 1:27:

> So God created humankind in his image,
>   in the image of God he created them;
>   male and female he created them.

We noted earlier the strikingly close connection in that passage between our creation in the image of God and our creation as sexual beings who are capable of love and marriage. The prophets and the New Testament writers are drawing on that same close connection when they speak about God's love as marital love. These descriptions make sense because the love that binds spouses together in a human marriage is an image of the divine love that fills God's heart to overflowing and reaches out to us in Christ. God's love and marital love are related to each other as a lamp is related to its reflected image in a mirror.

At least that may be the case some of the time. Every marriage has moments when the bond uniting spouses looks anything but divine! Genesis 1:27 points to the *potential* that exists for human marital love to become the image of God's love. But that potential is rarely realized in full. God's love for us is marital in the sense that God's love shows us what human marital love has the potential to become.

The Purposes of God

So here, in the biblical text, we find a picture emerging of God's intention and purpose for love, marriage, and sexuality. God gives us these good gifts in order to help us realize our creation in the divine image. Marriage is designed to help our human love grow into the image of God's own love for us.

Ephesians 5:21–33 fills in the details of this picture of God's intention for love and marriage, confirming that we are on the right track:

Be subject to one another out of reverence for Christ.

Wives, be subject to your husbands as you are to the Lord. . . .

Husbands, love your wives, just as Christ loved the church and gave himself up for her. . . . "For this reason a man will leave his father and mother and be joined to his wife, and the two will become one flesh." This is a great mystery, and I am applying it to Christ and the church. Each of you, however, should love his wife as himself, and a wife should respect her husband.

At first glance, the passage can be a little off-putting to modern readers, because it reflects a first-century understanding of marriage. In the time and culture where Ephesians was written, people took it utterly for granted that wives would be completely subordinate to their husbands. Modern understanding of marriage as an equal partnership lay centuries in the future. In accordance with the principles we identified for responsible biblical interpretation, we must be careful to read the passage in its historical context: It would be a grievous mistake to confuse the first-century Greco-Roman social conventions, which form the human, historical background of the passage, with the profound insight at its center about God's purposes for marriage.

Once we take into account the assumptions of the ancient, male-dominated culture in which the passage was written, we can see how it confirms God's intention for marriage to help us grow into the divine image of God's love for us. The author of the passage knows that the clearest picture we have of the love that fills God's hearts comes to us in the love Jesus shows as he reaches out to us. For this reason, the passage identifies the goal of marriage as growing into the kind of love that unites Jesus to the church. This growth in self-giving, Christ-like love is what it means for human beings to realize the potential of our creation in the image of God.

The author accommodates this picture to first-century assumptions about marriage. So when first-century wives grow in Christ-like self-giving, it means they lovingly subject themselves to their husband's direction. First-century husbands grow in self-giving love by becoming willing to sacrifice themselves completely for the sake of their wives. But shining through its Greco-Roman cultural assumptions, the message of Ephesians illumines the purpose of God to which all the other biblical references to marriage point: God gives human beings the gifts of love, marriage, and sexuality in order to help us grow into the image of Christ's self-giving love.

The Gift of Bodily Selves

We might think that this insight provides helpful guidance for only the emotional and spiritual dimensions of marriage. Love, affection, tender feelings, and the willingness to sacrifice for one's spouse are all important aspects of the marriage covenant. Jesus' love for us as individuals and as a church certainly gives us a noteworthy spiritual pattern and example to live into. But our concern has also been to understand the Bible's teaching about sexuality. When we speak about marriage as a school of Christ-like, self-giving love, a description that focuses only on spiritual and emotional love leaves out the more down-to-earth, bodily and sexual aspects of marriage that are important parts of the picture as well.

Christ's love for the church is not a disembodied, purely spiritual reality. The Gospel writers and the classical Christian creeds all emphasize that Jesus is a real, flesh-and-blood human being. The reality of the incarnation is a *bodily* reality. Jesus is the *incarnate* Son of God; the eternal Word of God became *flesh* and came to dwell among us.

Moreover, Jesus' loving gift of himself for us includes the gift of his body. Both the New Testament and the Christian liturgical tradition lift up Jesus' gift of his body as a critically important component of the Gospel witness. At the heart of the eucharistic celebration, the church repeats the words Jesus spoke to his disciples at the Last Supper: "This is my body, which is given for you" (Matt. 26:26; Mark 14:22; Luke 22:19; 1 Cor. 11:24).

The self-giving love of Jesus, which culminates with his sacrifice on the cross, represents a total gift of himself, body and spirit. Any human attempt to imitate or live into this kind of self-giving love will necessarily have both bodily and spiritual dimensions as well.

In the Gospels, Jesus does not shrink from encouraging his followers to imitate his bodily self-giving on the cross: "If any want to become my followers, let them deny themselves and take up their cross daily and follow me" (Matt. 16:24; Mark 8:34; Luke 9:23; see also Matt. 10:38). The church, from the very beginning, has honored the bodily self-giving of the martyrs, recognizing their sacrifices as luminous reflections of Christ's own self-giving love.

The self-giving of the martyrs, of course, involves a bodily gift of suffering and death similar to Jesus' sacrifice on the cross. How plausible is it to connect this sort of bodily sacrifice to the very different gift of bodies, one to another, that takes place between spouses in a marriage?

The ancient liturgies of the Eastern Orthodox Churches make exactly this connection between the bodily self-giving of Christ and the martyrs, and the bodily self-giving of spouses in a marriage. At the center of the marriage rite in the Orthodox Church is a "Crowning Ceremony," in which crowns are placed on the heads of the bride and groom. At first glance, we might view this as a way of emphasizing the special place of the young couple at the center of the celebration; they get to be king and queen for a day! But, in fact, the liturgy of the Crowning Ceremony is a deliberate effort to connect the bodily sacrifice of the martyrs with the gift of one's whole being to a beloved spouse, which takes place in a good marriage. These ceremonial crowns are symbols of the heavenly crowns worn by the martyrs who sacrificed their lives for the faith.[1] In the marriage context, they point to sanctifying death of the self, which takes place as spouses gradually learn to give themselves wholly to one another in mutual love and self-giving. And this complete self-gift includes the gift of bodies.

It is a testimony to the grace and generosity of God that we usually experience the bodily aspect of marital self-giving in joy and ecstasy, rather than in the pain and physical agony that marks the sacrifices of Christ and the holy martyrs. But this mercy of God should not blind us to the ways in which marriage, too, involves sacrifice: The self-giving communion of a good marriage leads us into the death of the self-enclosed ego and the offering up of the autonomous individual. It is only as we put to death these fallen, earthly aspects of ourselves that we are freed for growth into the divine image.

Here we see the deep truth the Bible points to with its mysterious recurring association between God's love for us and human, marital love. The physical, emotional, and covenantal aspects of the marriage bond all lead us toward the total gift of self to another human being. As we grow into this complete and mutual gift of self, which embraces every aspect of who we are, our lives become more faithful images and reflections of Christ's passionate gift of himself for us.

Our loving God wants us to experience the joy, passion, and mystery of this growth into the divine image. God blesses us with the gifts of love, marriage, and sexuality in order to help us grow more deeply into the image of Christ's self-giving love.

What about Single People?

I gave a presentation on God's purposes for love, marriage, and sexuality at a church conference. Afterward, an older pastor approached me looking concerned. "I have been single all my life," he said. "What you are saying about marriage makes it sound as if I have been left out of God's plan. Is my spiritual growth stunted unless I get married? I have a lot of married friends whose lives frankly don't look all that spiritual. I am trying to decide if what you say makes any sense."

The Bible's witness about marriage is impressive enough that it might lead us naturally toward the understanding that single people are at a spiritual disadvantage. The close proximity in Genesis 1:27 of our creation in the image of God and our creation as male and female could be interpreted to mean that human beings become fully reflective of the divine image only when they come together specifically as male and female in the bond of marriage.

One towering aspect of the New Testament's witness prevents us from reaching these conclusions, however, and that is the fact that *Jesus was single*. If marriage between a man and a woman were required for the divine image to be realized in human beings, then we would be forced to conclude, against the entire witness of the New Testament, that Jesus himself was a deficient example of the divine image in human beings.

This suggests that however great a potential help marriage might be in forming people in the image of God, the married state is not an essential requirement for it to happen. The Savior himself demonstrates the depths of love and spiritual development that can be achieved without it.

The apostle Paul, who was also a single person, lists spiritual advantages of single life in 1 Corinthians 7.[2] Paul points out how single people are able to live free from the daily distractions of relationship and household matters that inevitably accompany marriage and family life. This freedom, says Paul, provides a spiritual advantage to single persons by allowing them an opportunity to focus more consistently on serving God than is possible for their married counterparts (vv. 32–35). Paul is very careful, however, *not* to carry this insight forward to a conclusion that says truly dedicated Christians have a spiritual duty to refrain from getting married. To the contrary, Paul recognizes that God gives different vocations to different people, and that both married and single people have their own gifts from God (v. 7).

There is, of course, nothing forcing people to make use of the special gifts that God provides, whatever their station in life. Nearly everyone has encountered individuals whose lives show little outward evidence of spiritual blessing or growth in grace, whether they are single or married persons. Marriage and singleness each provide unique opportunities for growth into the divine image, but there is nothing automatic about the process. Both Christian marriage and Christian singleness require cultivation of the opportunities for growth in grace that God affords us.

Next Steps . . .

My survey of scriptural teaching on marriage led me to some strong conclusions about the purposes God had in mind in blessing human beings with the gifts of love, marriage, and sexuality. God intends for these gifts to help us grow into a deeper and richer experience of the joy, passion, and fulfillment that come with giving ourselves wholly to another in accordance with the pattern of Christ's self-giving love.

I realized that this understanding of God's purposes could provide a very helpful framework for guidance in a host of different situations where matters of relationships and sexuality were involved. The joy and fulfillment that accompany our growth into the image of Christ's self-giving are themselves the rich blessings God desires to confer on God's beloved children. The availability of God's blessing in any particular set of circumstances corresponds to the compatibility of those circumstances with self-giving love and with their ability to promote growth into a fuller reflection of the divine image.

My next task was to actually apply this framework to the question of same-sex marriage. Would same-gender relationships turn out to be fully compatible with the divine purposes for love, marriage, and sexuality I had uncovered? Does Scripture point to any specific features of such relationships that undermine their compatibility with God's purposes? And do same-gender relationships have the capacity to deepen our experience of God's blessings by nurturing us in the self-giving love of Christ? These are the questions that will occupy us in the next chapter.

CHAPTER 5

⌘⌘

SPECIAL BLESSINGS

Why Gay People Have an Honored Place in God's Heart

News of the young minister's suicide had shaken the small suburban town to its core. Pastor John seemed to have everything going for him: a thriving ministry, an engaging personality, a beautiful family. Everywhere people were responding to the news in shocked disbelief. Nobody could understand why he would take his own life. In a quiet moment with an older pastor who had been John's mentor and confidante over many years, I expressed my own puzzlement over the situation. The older man looked at me sadly and said, "John was gay. He thought he could deny it by marrying his wife and entering the ministry, but over the years his struggle grew worse and worse. I'm afraid in the end he didn't feel he could keep up the pretense any longer."

⌘⌘

John's case was one of a number of tragic situations I have encountered, where a devout gay or lesbian believer has tried valiantly to follow traditional church teaching and embrace the option of heterosexual marriage. These well-intended efforts to conform their lives to a church-prescribed, heterosexual pattern have very often resulted in heartache and tragedy, for both the individuals involved and their families. Becoming aware of the stakes involved led me to ask questions with a new urgency: Could God's blessing come to gay and lesbian believers who strive to live faithfully according to a different pattern? Is same-gender marriage a faithful possibility for people who seek to follow Jesus Christ?

My study of the Bible's teaching on love, marriage, and sexuality revealed that God's highest purpose in providing these gifts is to help people grow in their ability to give themselves completely to another person, following the pattern of Christ's self-giving love. It struck me as I considered this that there seemed to be nothing about this purpose that required an opposite-gender relationship.

A same-gender marriage appeared to afford the same or very similar opportunities for growth in love and grace and mutuality and for learning to give the whole of oneself to another person. And if God's purpose for marriage could be fulfilled in a gay marriage as well as a straight one, it made absolutely no sense to tell gay people that God's will for them could be fulfilled only in a heterosexual context or in celibacy. It appeared that gay people could find God's loving purposes for them fulfilled in and through a faithful, loving, lifelong commitment to a same-gender partner. But entertaining this conclusion immediately raised some questions.

The Question of Procreation

I realized that procreation was a feature of traditional, heterosexual marriage that had not received much attention in my study of the purposes of God. Is there something about a couple's ability to conceive and bear biological offspring that is essential to God's purposes for their marriage? Of course, parenthood is an option that is open to gay people, as the examples of a great many loving, adoptive gay parents amply illustrates. But ordinary biological procreation, apart from the involvement of a third party, is not a possibility for same-gender relationships. Does this make a difference in the ability of same-gender relationships to live into the purposes God has for love, marriage, and sexuality? Had I stacked the deck unwittingly in favor of gay marriage by leaving biological procreation off the list of God's essential purposes for marriage? What does the Bible have to say about this?

Procreation receives one mention in the passages at the beginning of Genesis that speak about God's creation of human beings as male and female:

> God blessed them, and God said to them, "Be fruitful and multiply, and fill the earth and subdue it."
>
> (Gen. 1:28)

Unlike many other biblical commands, God's directive to fill the earth is one that human beings have managed to carry out quite well! Indeed, one of the great challenges facing us as faithful stewards of God's creation is finding ways to sustain the large human population that now fills the earth, without doing irreparable damage to the planet. It would make no sense to insist that every single marriage needs to produce biological offspring in order to fulfill this charge from God. Its fulfillment by the human race as a whole has been well established for centuries.

Psalm 127:3–5 speaks of procreation, too, viewing offspring as a great blessing given by God. Conversely, barrenness is viewed as a heavy burden to bear; the Bible views childless marriages as tragic, especially for women (Gen. 30:22–23; Ruth 1:1–14). This is at least partly due to the male-dominated culture that forms the backdrop to the biblical writings. In that culture, women were heavily dependent on their husbands and, in later life, their sons for financial support. A marriage that failed to produce sons threatened a woman with a life of abject poverty following the death of her husband. Whatever the reason, childlessness has tragic dimensions in the view of the Old Testament writers, and if a previously barren woman gives birth, such an event is seen as a great blessing from God (Gen. 18:9–15; Judg. 13:3; 1 Sam. 1:9–20; Ps. 113:9; Isa. 54:1).

So the Bible clearly views procreation as a blessing, but nowhere is there even a hint suggesting that procreation is an essential requirement for a marriage to be considered legitimate in the eyes of God. No regulations appear anywhere in Scripture suggesting that infertile people or persons past the age of childbearing should refrain from getting married. Nowhere is there a suggestion that a marriage that continues childless somehow lacks legitimacy for that reason.

The obvious conclusion from all this is that while procreation is a wonderful gift with which God blesses some people, its absence does not undermine the value or legitimacy of particular marriages in God's eyes. The purposes of God that confer value and legitimacy on a marital union are evidently not dependent on the ability of that marriage to produce biological offspring. The lack of procreative ability poses no obstacle to the fulfillment of God's purposes in and through gay relationships.

The Significance of Adoption

The nonessential nature of biological procreation is further underscored in the New Testament, which elevates *adoption* to a high spiritual status and significance. Paul describes our incorporation into God's plan of redemption as a divine work in which the Holy Spirit makes us *adopted* children of God. This status as adopted children makes us co-inheritors of the coming kingdom along with Jesus (Rom. 8:14–25; Gal. 4:4–7).

We have suggested that God's highest purpose for love, marriage, and sexuality is to form us into the kind of self-giving love that binds Christ to the church. Nurturing children has the ability to bring out that kind of love in us, at least on our better days as parents. But that will be true whether children are biological or adopted. The New Testament quite pointedly describes the love that binds us to God in terms of the bond that exists between *adopted* children and a loving parent. There is nothing essential about a couple's *biological* offspring that makes them better suited than adoptive children for accomplishing God's purpose of teaching us to give ourselves in love.

In short, whatever role we accord to the care and nurture of children in promoting God's purposes for love, marriage, and sexuality, it is clear that these purposes can be advanced every bit as well when the children are adopted as when they are the biological offspring of their parents. Since gay people are fully capable of fulfilling the role of adoptive parents, our conclusion stands: a particular couple's ability to bear biological offspring has no bearing on whether or not their relationship can embody God's highest purpose for marriage as expressed in Scripture. There is no reason that same-gender relationships cannot advance and embody God's purposes for love, marriage, and sexuality as well as straight ones can.

Male and Female Anatomy

Now, at this point, some people will object on the basis of what I call the argument from plumbing: "Just look at the particulars of male and female anatomy," they say. "It is perfectly obvious from the way human bodies are constructed that men and women are meant for one another. Any attempt to deny this or live as if it were not true makes a mockery of God's work of creation."[1] The bumper-sticker form of this argument says, "God created Adam and Eve, not Adam and Steve."

Proponents of this argument sometimes appeal to the Genesis account of God's creation of human beings as male and female to support what they are saying:

> So God created humankind in his image,
>   in the image of God he created them;
>   male and female he created them. . . .

SPECIAL BLESSINGS / 61

Therefore a man leaves his father and his mother and clings
to his wife, and they become one flesh.

(Gen. 1:27; 2:24)

Opponents of gay relationships sometimes claim that these
Genesis passages point to a "one-flesh union" that is the natural
outcome of our creation as male and female.

Not content to limit their case to Genesis, these critical
voices also try to enlist Jesus in their argument, even though
Jesus never once touches on the issue of same-gender relationships in all the recorded teaching we have from him. But in
Matthew 19:3-6, Jesus quotes these Genesis passages about our
creation as male and female, and some would say that Jesus'
citation of these passages must mean he endorses traditional
marriage and therefore opposes same-gender relationships.

Unfortunately for these critics, this argument depends on a
logical fallacy. Jesus' obvious approval of traditional, heterosexual marriage in no way implies that he would necessarily disapprove of same-gender relationships. That would be like saying
if a person enjoys having ice cream for dessert, this proves she
must not like apple pie.

Such claims are also wildly anachronistic. As we will see in
chapters 6 and 7, same-sex marriage simply wasn't on the radar
screen as a topic of discussion in New Testament times. Though
other, quite different, same-gender behaviors receive mention
at various points in Scripture, Jesus himself utters not a single
word about them.

This attempt to claim Jesus' quotations from Genesis for
the modern debate about gay marriage is actually quite ironic,
because the conversation in which they occur is about heterosexual divorce. In Matthew 19, Jesus quotes Genesis in order
to urge strict limitations on divorce: "Therefore what God has
joined together, let no one separate" (v. 6). Christ's disciples recognize this as a very difficult teaching, and Jesus himself admits
a few verses later that it is not for everyone (vv. 10–12).

Encouraged by Jesus' admission, a great many churches
have become more open and accepting of divorced persons, as

they have learned to interpret this teaching in light of the Bible's broader teachings about grace and forgiveness. It makes little sense, therefore, to lift Jesus' Genesis quotations out of context to support a very strict position about gay relationships—which he never addresses—while softening his actual teaching about heterosexual divorce![2]

While Jesus' citation of Genesis doesn't appear relevant to our consideration of gay marriage, we do need to acknowledge that the argument from plumbing points to something real. Male and female bodies clearly do complement each other. And as a consequence, the union of male and female is clearly established as the majority pattern for love and marriage across the whole span of human history. It would be silly to try to claim otherwise. But acknowledging this obvious fact of human experience hardly settles the gay marriage question.

The mere existence of a majority pattern does *not* mean that all departures from this pattern are automatically off-limits or condemned. To cite an everyday example that illustrates the logic of this: Most people I have surveyed do not like anchovies on their pizza. Consequently a great many pizza restaurant menus affirm this majority pattern by not even offering anchovies as an option among their list of possible pizza toppings. But just because a well-established majority pattern for pizza toppings exists does not mean that people like me, who think an anchovy pizza is something heavenly, are automatically wrong. The mere existence of a busy thoroughfare does not mean that a road less traveled is therefore illegitimate. The less-traveled paths need to be evaluated on their own merits.

The argument from plumbing goes astray in its unstated assumption that the mere existence of a majority path for love and marriage automatically means that alternative paths are illegitimate or out of bounds. Putting the question in religious terms, we might ask: Does God's creation of male and female bodies in biological correspondence to each other mean that God's condemnation *automatically* falls on alternative patterns of life like same-sex unions? This conclusion seems especially doubtful in light of our finding that same-sex unions are equally as capable as their heterosexual counterparts of fulfilling the highest revealed purposes God has in mind for love and marriage.

Proponents of the argument from plumbing sometimes appeal to what is "natural" for human beings. And it is certainly a fact of nature that a majority of human beings — though by no means all — come into this world as anatomically either male or female.[3] But anatomy isn't everything. Human beings are composed of bodies and spirits. A great many gay people tell stories about coming to realize they were simply incapable of romantic and sexual feelings for persons of the opposite gender. The majority path of traditional, heterosexual marriage was not open to them. These emotional and spiritual realities, no less than our bodies, are surely a part of our makeup as human beings. Does it make sense to claim that the bodies we are born with are part of "nature," while the spirits and affections we are born with are not? And if human spirits draw certain people in a different direction from what anatomy suggests, is there any justification in Scripture for saying that physical, bodily reality ought to trump spiritual reality? It is hard to find a single word supporting this privileging of the body, rather than offering equal value to both body and spirit.

On top of all this, the attempt to read directions for human morality from what occurs "naturally" is a dubious enterprise. Recognizably male and female anatomy occur widely in the world of nature, and the complementary function of these anatomical features is readily observable. But human beings should not imitate uncritically the testimony of nature. My favorite example of this is the female preying mantis, whose natural mating behavior includes eating the head of her male counterpart during sex! Basing human morality on what occurs in nature is clearly a hazardous business.

One of the most striking responses I ever heard to the charge that same-gender marriages involve using bodies in ways that are not "natural" came from Justin Lee, whose own struggles to come to terms with his identity as both a gay man and a Christian led to the formation in 2001 of the Gay Christian Network.[4] In response to a question about natural and unnatural activity,

Justin asked his hearers to consider the case of deaf people. Deaf people, like gay people, come into this life with a catalog of gifts and abilities that differs in certain respects from the majority population. The majority takes for granted that they will be able to marry a person of the opposite sex, but this possibility is closed off for gay people. Similarly, the majority takes for granted that speech and hearing can be used for communication, but this possibility is closed off for deaf people. This does not mean that deaf people miss out on life, however, because they have found alternative ways of using their bodies to accommodate the different set of abilities they have been born with; they might use sign language. Justin went on to observe that communicating with one's hands isn't really "natural." It doesn't always work as smoothly as communicating via speech and hearing: sign language requires a direct line of sight, and the speaker's hands can't be occupied with something else at the time. One might even argue that communicating in this way is not what hands were created to do. But nobody condemns deaf people for using their hands in this "unnatural" way. To the contrary; we celebrate and support this alternative use of their bodies, which allows deaf people to fully participate in significant aspects of human experience that would otherwise be out of reach for them. Why can we not also celebrate with gay people, asked Justin, who have found their own alternative ways of participating in the profoundly human experiences of love, marriage, and sexuality within the context of the different set of abilities they have been born with?[5]

Biblical Support for the Road Less Traveled

However persuasive such common-sense appeals might seem, however, I realized that I would need biblical grounding for a case supporting departures from the majority pattern for human life. The creation texts in Genesis lay out this majority pattern quite clearly; God created human beings male and female. A man leaves his father and mother and clings to his wife. This is a normative pattern for human existence set forth at the very beginning of the scriptural witness. What do we make of lives that depart from this norm?

I recognized that the key question I needed to answer was this: Would it be in character for the God of the Bible to establish a standard, majority pattern for human life, but then *also* to confer blessing on lives that depart from this pattern? Is the God revealed to us in Scripture a God who blesses the road less traveled in addition to the major thoroughfare, or does God prefer to work through a single, majority norm?

These questions arose for me out of the witness of Genesis, and I found the beginnings of an answer taking shape in Genesis as well. Genesis 2:5–17 presents the outlines of the standard plan God intends for human beings to follow ever after. God instructs "the man" in the way of obedience, establishes life in Eden, and charges humans to till and keep this garden paradise that God has provided.

The expected plan at creation was for Adam and Eve to continue in loving and faithful obedience to God, and to fill the earth with their equally loving, faithful, and obedient offspring. But a single chapter later, in Genesis 3, we see how that standard plan winds up on the rocks. Adam and Eve choose a path of disobedience and rebel against the God who gave them life. The alternative path they choose leads to estrangement from God, from each other, and from the earth God has charged them to care for (vv. 8–19).

From that point on, the entire Bible is the story of God repeatedly bringing redemption, blessing, and salvation to a fallen world that stands firmly outside the plan and pattern of God's original intention. So claiming that God blesses only the standard pattern that appears in the creation stories in Genesis would require us to dismiss almost the entire witness of the Bible, from Genesis 3 through the very last chapter of the book of Revelation! The good news of God's compassion and blessing, poured out on a fallen world that has departed from the standard pattern of God's intention, would be utterly lost.

What is true of the whole appears also in the details. Over and over again the pages of Scripture witness to a God who delights in confounding standard expectations and conferring blessing outside the conventional, majority ways of doing things.

The standard expectations coming out of the creation accounts in Genesis would be for God's chosen people to arise from Adam and Eve's naturally conceived children. These strong and healthy offspring would all be descended from the attractive and vigorous young couple God originally set in the Garden of Eden. Instead of that, however, God ostentatiously highlights the *nonstandard* nature of the world's redemption by bringing forth the chosen people from Sarah and Abraham: an infertile, elderly couple who are long past the years of natural childbearing (Gen. 12:1-9; 15:1–18:15; 21:1–20).

One would expect the chosen people arising from Abraham and Sarah's miraculous offspring to become strong and prosperous and independent. A people who were the recipients of God's blessing would surely do well for themselves in the world. Yet these expectations wind up on the rocks. The account beginning with Genesis 37 and culminating with Exodus 1 tells the story of God's chosen people falling into slavery and captivity in the land of Egypt. The extended story that follows, of Moses and the exodus, is all about God's execution of an alternative plan, outside the realm of standard expectations, to bring blessing to God's people.

In fact, Scripture repeatedly demonstrates that clinging too tightly to conventional expectations and normal ways of working can make us blind to what the God of the Bible is actually doing. In the time of Christ, the scribes and Pharisees thought they knew perfectly well from their reading of Scripture that the Messiah would rally the armies of Israel and cast off the shackles of Roman occupation. Clinging too tightly to these standard expectations led many of these religious authorities to completely overlook God's actual redemption of the world through the unanticipated appearance of a suffering and crucified Messiah.

The letter to the Hebrews emphasizes how Jesus was crucified outside the walls of Jerusalem, and lifts this up as a symbol of the way God's work in Jesus takes place outside the entire structure of conventional religious expectations and institutions (13:10–14). God's redemption of the world through the cross of Christ is an alternative arrangement that stands dramatically apart from God's normal, expected ways of working through the holy temple and the holy priesthood in the holy city of Jerusalem. Jesus' early disciples realized that no normal, conventional religious structure, arrangement, or institution could match the blessing God had poured out on the world through this unconventional, alternative path of Jesus' cross and resurrection. The road less traveled turns out to be the pathway of redemption in the Bible's witness!

The God of the Bible delights in defying conventional arrangements, confounding established patterns, and pouring out blessing by surprising means in unexpected places. It would be utterly in character for this God to provide blessing outside the conventional patterns and expectations set forth in the Genesis accounts of human creation as male and female. God's blessing of same-gender marriages is entirely consistent with the pattern of God's working, witnessed to by the entire Bible, Old and New Testaments.

The Conversion of the Gentiles

Scripture provides no concrete examples of God blessing same-sex marriages. This is because mutually loving, egalitarian marriages between gay partners were simply not an available option for ordinary people during the times when the Bible was written. But Scripture does provide striking examples of God providing blessing in ancient situations that depart from majority patterns in ways that bear significant resemblance to contemporary gay marriage. A striking example comes from the book of Acts.

Acts 10:1–11:18 presents remarkable testimony to a Spirit-led revolution in the early Christian community, which resulted in the inclusion of the Gentiles in the ranks of the previously all-Jewish church. Before this revolution took place, faithful Christians looked on the Gentiles as despised and unholy outsiders.

The reasons for this view were understandable: Gentiles did not follow the biblical Law that represented God's revealed will for the chosen people. Gentiles were regarded as so unclean and religiously contaminated that faithful Jews and Jewish Christians—including Jesus' original disciples—were prohibited from even sharing a meal with them. Traditional Jewish attitudes toward the Gentiles bore a significant resemblance to the attitudes toward gay people that are reflected in the traditional condemnations: The Gentiles were a people whom faithful religious believers saw as standing outside the bounds of biblical Law; the Gentiles were clearly condemned by their lack of faithfulness to the biblical commands, traditionally understood.

In a shocking and unexpected development, however, the Holy Spirit started leading even these unholy and unclean people toward faithful devotion to Christ. This movement of the Holy Spirit among the Gentiles was supported by an equally powerful movement of the Spirit among the early church leaders, beginning with Peter. Through dreams, visions, and angelic messengers, God convinces Peter to recognize the legitimacy of the Gentiles' faith in Jesus and to welcome them into the church. For those early church leaders, this was the ultimate "nonstandard" route to God's blessing!

But the really surprising feature of this story is what does *not* occur in it. When the Gentiles come into the church, there is *no* requirement for them to repent of being Gentiles. These new believers remain who they are; they continue to live outside traditional understandings of biblical Law, as they always have. Their baptism and conversion do *not* mean that they must now adopt the standard path and start to follow Jewish law with the majority of Jesus' followers up to that point. As Paul puts it in his letter to the Galatians, "We ourselves are Jews by birth and not Gentile sinners; yet we know that a person is justified not by the works of the law but through faith in Jesus Christ" (2:15–16).

This is a major theme of the New Testament, especially Paul's letters. Through Christ, God has made available a new faith-based path to divine blessing and salvation entirely apart from the previously existing norms and standard expectations.

This blessing is open even to people like the Gentiles who do not follow traditional understandings of the biblical Law. This proclamation serves as a powerful biblical precedent for our suggestion that God's blessing also extends to gay people whose marriages and relationships stand apart from traditional understandings of biblical Law.

It would be utterly consistent with this biblical precedent for God to do an end run around the requirements of biblical Law, as traditionally understood, in order to bless and welcome this previously despised and alienated group of gay and lesbian people into the fellowship of Christ's flock. The evidence that God has in fact done this echoes the New Testament story of the Gentiles: the Holy Spirit is actively at work in the lives of lesbian and gay believers, filling their hearts with the love of Jesus.

It is important to note here that when God allows the Gentiles to enter the Christian fold outside traditional observances of the Law, this does not mean that the church is now governed by an "anything goes" attitude. The Gentiles do not miss out on the opportunity to grow in grace and discipleship as part of their Christian walk. Instead, the Holy Spirit helps them to advance in love and faithfulness by a different path than was marked out by traditional understandings of biblical Law. Paul even argues that this alternative path to faithfulness is a superior one. He calls the written Law as traditionally understood "the law of sin and death," acutely aware that his own devotion to this written law had led him to oppose Christ and persecute the church prior to his conversion. Listen to how Paul contrasts the two:

> There is therefore now no condemnation for those who are in Christ Jesus. For the law of the Spirit of life in Christ Jesus has set you free from the law of sin and of death.
>
> (Rom. 8:1–2)

For those whose lives stand at odds with traditional understanding of the written, biblical Law, God has provided a superior, Spirit-guided path for them to grow in grace and faithfulness.

The Road Less Traveled
in Sexual Matters

The conversion of the Gentiles provides a dramatic example of God's readiness to recognize and bless patterns of discipleship that follow alternative, less-traveled paths that stand apart from majority patterns of fulfilling biblical Law. In our contemporary wrestling with issues surrounding gay marriage, however, we are dealing with questions that have to do specifically with love and sexuality. I started wondering if there was anything in the Bible that specifically suggested a willingness on God's part to bless less-traveled paths in the area of sexual life. When I started looking for one, I couldn't believe how significant the example I found turned out to be.

Every year during the Christmas season, faithful Christians ponder the angel Gabriel's annunciation to the Virgin Mary (Luke 1:26–38). Gabriel tells Mary of God's desire that she become the mother of the Christ child. In popular piety, Mary's virginity is a symbol of purity, and rightly so. But to focus on this aspect alone is to miss the truly stunning significance of Christ's conception in the womb of the virgin.

In point of fact, young Mary is an unwed bride-to-be, and if Gabriel's message to her turns out to be true, she will be pregnant long before her marriage is consummated. The situation Gabriel describes to her will inevitably cause dark clouds of scandal and immorality to overshadow her life. Those dark clouds promise to bring not only shame and dishonor to her; there is also a real possibility that they will turn lethal. Traditional Old Testament law prescribed death by stoning as the penalty for a woman's unfaithfulness to a formally betrothed husband!

The Gospel of Matthew reports what happens when Joseph discovers that the woman he is engaged to is already pregnant. Joseph, being a righteous man, elects to treat this personal humiliation with mercy; he will not press charges or expose Mary to public disgrace but instead plans to send Mary away quietly to fend for herself (Matt. 1:18–19). Mary's prospects still look quite bleak. For a disgraced woman, alienated from her family in this way, such a fate could very well lead to a life of either begging or prostitution as the only viable options for survival.

But Matthew's Gospel also reports that an angel of the Lord intervenes in the situation at just this point, appearing to Joseph in a dream and convincing him of Mary's innocence. The angel persuades Joseph to move forward with his plans to take Mary as his wife (vv. 20–25).

The remarkable thing about this episode, as presented in the New Testament, is that it all takes place as the deliberate plan of God. Could there be a more striking sign of God's intention to identify with the sexually marginalized? The omnipotent Lord of the entire universe could easily have chosen to be born within the wholesome confines of a stable, traditional family. Christ could have entered the world through the sexual path of the respectable majority. Yet when God comes to us, the eternal Logos assumes human flesh deliberately and dramatically and scandalously outside the majority norms and structures of traditional marriage.

This is not to say that all sexual norms are overturned in the Scriptures and that anything goes. As we saw in chapter 4, God has particular purposes in mind for love, marriage, and sexuality; and some patterns of life are vastly more compatible with those purposes than others. But it would be hard to imagine a clearer message about majority and minority patterns than the one that emerges from the circumstances of Jesus' own birth. God specializes and delights in bringing forth blessing from situations that stand outside the bounds of traditional, majority patterns of life, including majority patterns of love and marriage. It would be hard to imagine any clearer indication of God's willingness to bless minority patterns like same-gender marriage, especially since those patterns are fully capable of fulfilling God's highest purposes for love, marriage, and sexuality.

The Journey So Far . . .

My study of the Bible now had me completely convinced that gay relationships are fully as capable as heterosexual ones of fulfilling God's scripturally revealed intentions for love, marriage, and sexuality. The ability of a marriage to support the growth of two people together into the image of Christ's complete, self-giving love does not depend in any essential way on the gender of the partners.

I considered carefully whether the absence of biological procreative ability or the allegedly "unnatural" aspects of gay relationships would somehow undermine their ability to fulfill God's purposes. I concluded, on the basis of both common sense and scriptural witness, that these distinctive characteristics of same-sex relationships posed no obstacle to the fulfillment of God's purposes for them.

Finally, I embraced the honest recognition that gay marriage does stand outside the majority pattern for marriage that is set forth in the opening chapters of Genesis. But I also found a strong and consistent witness throughout the Scriptures testifying to God's willingness to provide blessing in situations that stand apart from such majority patterns. The Bible gave me every reason to believe that the blessings God pours out through the gifts of love, marriage, and sexuality are richly available to gay couples, just as they are to straight ones.

As hopeful as these results were, however, I was still aware that the scriptural fragments that support the traditional condemnations were still "out there." As a Christian who subscribes to a strong doctrine of biblical authority, I was very uncomfortable saying that these texts were outdated or mistaken or that they could be ignored. I knew that in order to fully embrace the hopeful conclusions I had turned up about God's blessing of same-sex relationships, I would need to find a way to positively incorporate these traditional fragments into the big picture of the Bible's witness. This is the task we will turn to in the next chapter.

CHAPTER 6

⟨◦⟩◦⟨◦⟩

RECLAIMING
THE WITNESSES 1

*Making Sense of the
Old Testament Fragments*

I am in a lab room of a local hospital, waiting to have my blood drawn for a routine physical. The staff nurse is making small talk as she ties the rubber tourniquet around my arm. "Oh, so you're a writer are you? That's very interesting! What kind of things do you write?" I find I can wind up in very long conversations telling people I am writing a book about gay marriage, so I try to satisfy her with a generic answer, telling her that I write about religion. She isn't satisfied with a vague answer, however. As she prepares her glass vials and alcohol swab, she asks, "And what are you working on now?" As hesitant as I am to bring up a controversial topic with a person who is brandishing a large needle, it is early morning, I've had no coffee, and a clever way of deflecting the conversation eludes me. "I'm writing a book about gay marriage" I blurt out. "Ohhhhhh," she replies, eyeing me skeptically. "I'm not at all sure about that. I know there's that stuff in the Bible . . ."

⟨◦⟩◦⟨◦⟩

Sooner or later I knew I was going to have to deal with "that stuff in the Bible." I was greatly encouraged by the results of my biblical survey. I had uncovered a number of scripturally grounded reasons for believing that the traditional condemnations of same-gender relationships were mistaken (ch. 1). I had come to see how same-gender relationships were fully capable of fulfilling God's purposes for love, marriage, and sexuality (chs. 4 and 5). All the results of my Scripture study were strongly pointing toward the acceptability of same-sex relationships in God's eyes.

Yet here was this group of seven passages, "the fragment texts" I called them, which appeared to speak a very negative word about homosexuality (Gen. 19:1–29; Judg. 19:1–30; Lev. 18:22; 20:13; Jude 5–7; Rom. 1:18–27; 1 Cor. 6:9–17; 1 Tim. 1:10). The situation felt like having a jigsaw puzzle nearly completed, with only a single piece remaining to put in place. Except when I tried to add that final piece, it didn't fit with the rest of the puzzle! This was a strong indication that something was wrong with my understanding of the fragment texts.

A number of my liberal Christian friends chose to simply ignore these passages or dismiss them as outdated or mistaken. But disregarding portions of Scripture because I was uncomfortable with what they said seemed unwise to me. If we did that on a regular basis, we would undermine Scripture's ability to call us into question in situations where our lives might really need correcting. I felt that there had to be some more faithful way of understanding these passages that would be consistent with the other biblical results I had uncovered. But what could it be?

The Importance of Context

One time-honored principle for faithful interpretation of the Bible says that we need to keep in mind the historical and biblical contexts of passages we are trying to understand. An old joke illustrates the hazards of reading our modern worldview into the biblical text:

Q: What was the favorite automotive brand of the early church leaders?
A: They preferred Hondas:

> It seemed good unto us, being assembled with one *accord*, to send chosen men unto you with our beloved Barnabas and Paul.
>
> (Acts 15:25, KJV, emphasis added)

Finding references to the modern-day Honda Accord in the biblical text is such an outlandish historical mistake that it makes us laugh (or perhaps groan). But there are other, more subtle ways we can distort the Bible's meaning by reading into it features of our modern world.

I started reading an award-winning historical study by Finnish scholar Martti Nissinen about same-sex practices in the biblical world.[1] I was surprised to discover that "homosexuality" is a distinctly modern concept that was unknown to the ancient world. There is no single word in the original biblical languages that translates into "gay" or "homosexual" as we understand the terms, and the biblical world has no corresponding concept of a person's sexual orientation.[2] The notion that the Bible would condemn a person for having a same-sex orientation was apparently an anachronism on a par with finding references to Honda Accords in Scripture.

However, even without a concept of sexual orientation, the fragment passages certainly seemed to disapprove of certain behaviors. I realized I couldn't just assume what those behaviors were, based on my familiarity with same-sex relationships in today's world. I started wondering what, exactly, these passages were objecting to, if it was clear historically that the writers had no concept of gay people who partner together as a way of living out their sexual orientation.

A good starting place, I thought, was to let the Bible tell me what sorts of behavior these passages were objecting to. Some of the fragment passages actually did present fairly detailed and lengthy descriptions of the behaviors at issue. At the top of this list of descriptions was the story of Sodom and Gomorrah in Genesis 19:1–29.

Genesis 19:1-29

The setting for the story actually appears in the previous chapter:

> Then the LORD said, "How great is the outcry against Sodom and Gomorrah and how very grave their sin! I must go down and see whether they have done altogether according to the outcry that has come to me; and if not, I will know.
>
> (Gen. 18:20–21)

In order to carry out this divine fact-finding mission, God sends two angels, who travel to Sodom in the guise of ordinary men. Abraham's nephew Lot, who lives in Sodom, spots the two strangers entering the city, and in a customary gesture of ancient Near Eastern hospitality, he invites them to spend the night at his home, entertaining them with a feast.

At this point the story turns dark:

> But . . . the men of Sodom, both young and old, all the people to the last man, surrounded the house; and they called to Lot, "Where are the men who came to you tonight? Bring them out to us, so that we may know them."
>
> (19:4–5)

"That we may know them" is of course the biblical euphemism for sexual activity, and it is clear from the context that the crowd intends to abuse the visitors. As the story unfolds, Lot goes out of his house to plead with the gathered mob, explaining that he has committed himself to providing a safe shelter for these wayfarers. In a strange and repellent twist of the story, Lot even offers to send out his two daughters as a substitute offering to appease the mob (v. 8). This gesture at once illustrates the importance of the code of hospitality that Lot is trying to uphold, and the shockingly low status of women in the bronze-age society that is the backdrop of the story.

Fortunately for the women, the members of the mob want no part of this offer. They respond that Lot, too, is an alien in the city, and they promise to dispense even worse treatment to him than to the two strangers (v. 9). These details are important, because they indicate that the motivation of the mob is not lust but hatred toward outsiders. The men of Sodom intend to inflict dramatic punishment on Lot's guests in order to ensure that their city never has to tolerate the presence of foreigners within its walls.

As the remainder of the story unfolds, the two angels rescue Lot by miraculously striking the mob with blindness. After this the Lord warns Lot and his family to flee the wicked city, and both Sodom and its neighboring city of Gomorrah perish when the Lord rains down fire from heaven on them.

This story has often been used to justify across-the-board condemnations of any and all forms of same-gender activity. But the particular behavior that is judged so negatively in the passage turns out to be homosexual gang rape used as a weapon against foreigners! I realized that there was absolutely nothing in this story to contradict any of the conclusions I had come to about God's readiness to bless loving, committed same-sex relationships. The brutal, hate-filled behavior that is punished in the Sodom story *deserves* to be punished, whether it occurs in a heterosexual or a same-sex context. The sexual violence depicted there is utterly contrary to God's intended purposes for love, marriage, and sexuality that had emerged from my survey of the broader witness of Scripture. To my surprise, I found I could fully affirm the negative judgment of the Sodom story. But this negative judgment against gang rape had no implications at all for the loving, covenanted partnerships and marriages that were the subject of my investigations.

Judges 19

The story of Sodom is not an isolated episode. Judges 19, which has also been used to condemn same-sex relationships across the board, presents a similar story. In the Judges passage, we find a male Levite and his concubine traveling far from home. Once again, the travelers receive welcome and hospitality along the way from an old man who resides in the city of Gibeah, in the territory of Benjamin. Once again a hostile mob gathers outside the man's house, demanding that he surrender the male foreigner so that they can abuse him sexually (v. 22). As in the Sodom account, the host, in desperation, offers women from the household in order to appease the hostile citizens.

The Gibeah episode takes a different turn, however, when the mob accepts the man's offer. They punish the Levite traveler by raping and abusing his concubine, leaving her dead on the man's doorstep the following morning.

Without hesitation, the Bible labels these actions by the men of Gibeah a horrific and vile crime. Their rape and murder of the Levite's concubine serve, in fact, to precipitate a war, as the armies of the surrounding Israelite tribes gather to inflict punishment on the whole territory of Benjamin, in which the city of Gibeah resides (ch. 20).

The account illustrates especially well how little sense it makes to take biblical judgments against homosexual gang rape (or the threat of it, as in the Gibeah story) and use them as the basis for across-the-board condemnation of loving, faithful same-sex partnerships. If we were to carry that logic through consistently, we would have to condemn heterosexual marriage as well: The Bible rightly views the heterosexual gang rape carried out by the men of Gibeah as a terrible crime. Does this imply a negative judgment against all forms of heterosexual activity, including loving, faithful marriages? I found it baffling and shocking to realize that a substantial portion of the Christian community has been willing to embrace exactly this sort of convoluted logic in applying these passages to gay people.

Once again, I found I could fully affirm the negative judgments against rape contained in the Gibeah story. Such actions are totally opposed to God's desire that our sexuality help us grow in Christ-like love and mutuality. This is true whether the rape in question is heterosexual or homosexual. But these reasonable and understandable condemnations of rape do not cast the slightest shadow of judgment over loving and faithful marriages. And once again, I could embrace the message of this fragment passage without any contradiction of my positive conclusions about same-sex marriages.

Leviticus 18:22 and 20:13

I started to wonder if this pattern would continue with the other fragment passages. Would reading them in their historical and literary contexts also reveal quite reasonable and understandable judgments against terrible behaviors that have no connection to committed, loving relationships?

Leviticus 18:22 and 20:13 are similar passages that have often been used to justify a blanket condemnation of same-gender activity:

> You shall not lie with a male as with a woman; it is an abomination.
>
> (18:22)

> If a man lies with a male as with a woman, both of them have committed an abomination.
>
> (20:13)

I had seen with the Genesis and Judges fragments how little sense it made to take passages that were pronouncing judgment against rape and to act as if they had anything to say about marriage. Could something similar be happening with the traditional use of these fragments from Leviticus? When the ancient Israelites heard this reference to a man lying with another male, what circumstances would they associate with such an action?

In trying to figure out what the Leviticus passages referred to, it made sense to rely on the testimony of the Bible itself. Genesis 19 and Judges 19 both identified male-male sexual activity with violent gang rape. Surveying the entire Old Testament, I could find only one other unambiguous description of males lying with males: This involved male cult prostitutes, whose activities played a role in the idolatrous worship rites of pagan tribes surrounding the nation of Israel. Reference to these cult prostitutes can be found in Deuteronomy 23:17; 1 Kings 14:24; 15:12; 22:46; and 2 Kings 23:7.

My findings from this survey of the Old Testament lined up with what I was reading in Nissinen, who was using the results of history and archaeology in addition to the direct witness of Scripture: the world of the biblical writers had nothing that remotely resembles the loving, egalitarian, committed gay marriages and partnerships that we know today. To read scriptural passages referring to same-gender sexual activity and think they apply to modern gay relationships is very much like finding references to Honda Accords in the Bible: It imports features of our modern world into the biblical narrative that simply didn't exist in the biblical world.

As we found in our consideration of Genesis 19 and Judges 19, the fractured logic that results when we read marriage into these texts comes into sharper focus when we consider heterosexual examples as well. The pagan cults that tempted the Israelites during this time in their history involved the activity of female as well as male prostitutes, which means their worship rites featured both heterosexual and homosexual prostitution (Deut. 23:17–18). We do not take the Bible's condemnations of heterosexual temple prostitution and conclude from it that heterosexual marriage is ungodly. Why on earth would we think such a leap made sense in the case of gay people?

The book of Leviticus contains confirmation that the prohibitions it contains are specifically targeted at the idolatrous practices of the Canaanite tribes who occupied the territories surrounding Israel. The references to males lying with males occur as part of a long list of prohibitions that concludes with the following word from God:

> You shall keep all my statutes and all my ordinances. . . . You shall not follow the practices of the nation that I am driving out before you. Because they did all these things, I abhorred them. . . . I am the LORD your God; I have separated you from the peoples.
>
> (20:22–24)

The prohibitions in Leviticus were designed to prevent the Israelites from falling into very specific idolatrous activities practiced by the pagan peoples who had previously occupied the land.

This does not mean Leviticus has nothing to say to us today, however. Once again, I was finding that when I understood their context better, the prohibitions in Leviticus started to make a lot of sense. When the ancient Israelites heard references to males lying with other males, their thoughts would have turned to gang rape and similarly violent forms of sexual aggression on the one hand or to temple prostitution on the other. It is as true today as it was thousands of years ago that neither gang rape nor cultic prostitution furthers God's purposes for marriage and sexuality! Faithful twenty-first century Christians would not affirm even heterosexual forms of such activities. Reading these passages from Genesis, Judges, and Leviticus in their proper historical context allowed me to wholeheartedly affirm their condemnations of violent and idolatrous sexual behaviors without casting the slightest doubt on my positive conclusions about same-sex marriage. I was starting to feel very encouraged!

Ambiguous Cases in the Old Testament

As I surveyed the Old Testament, I came across three passages that might be seen as suggesting same-sex activity, but they contained no explicit reference to it. The first of these ambiguous examples is the story of the drunkenness of Noah in Genesis 9:20–29. In this story, Noah consumed way too much wine and passed out in his tent, dead drunk. While Noah lay unconscious, his son Ham came in and "saw the nakedness of his father" (v. 22). Surprisingly, this caused great scandal among Ham's brothers and resulted in Noah pronouncing a curse on Ham's offspring. Given the severity of the family's reaction to this incident, there is some reason to think that the reference to Ham "seeing" his father's nakedness may be a euphemism for a more serious sexual offense.

Even if that theory is correct, however, there is no reason to think the condemnation of Ham's action has any bearing on the question of gay marriage. The judgment in this passage falls on Ham's incestuous violation of his drunk and helpless father. As in the Sodom and Gibeah stories, this encounter isn't even remotely comparable to a marriage relationship. Once again, I found I could heartily endorse the negative judgment of the behaviors hinted at in the passage. But it would require extremely convoluted and faulty logic to say that because the passage condemns sexual abuse and incest, it must also be condemning marriage! Such a leap would make no sense in a heterosexual context; neither does it hold water when applied to same-gender relationships.

My survey of the Old Testament turned up two other stories that might contain hints of same-gender activity, if we read between the lines. The first of these is the description of the relationship between Ruth and Naomi, which is described in the book of Ruth, chapter 1. The second is the bond between David and Jonathan, which is described in 1 Samuel 18–23 and 2 Samuel 1.

These two relationships reflect the kind of caring, mutually devoted bond that we might associate with a loving marriage. Ruth's loving devotion to her mother-in-law, Naomi, involves a faithful, lifelong commitment. Likewise, 1 Samuel 18:1 reports that "the soul of Jonathan was bound to the soul of David, and Jonathan loved him as his own soul." When Jonathan falls in battle, David's heartbroken lament over the loss of his beloved companion is truly striking:

> I am distressed for you, my brother Jonathan;
> greatly beloved were you to me;
>> your love to me was wonderful,
>> passing the love of women.

(2 Sam. 1:26)

The Bible contains no explicit reference to sexual activity as part of either of these relationships, but the depth of love and devotion described in each instance has led some commentators to speculate that these were more than just platonic friendships.

Whether or not we find such speculations plausible, it is certainly the case that the bonds between these two same-gender "couples" have more features in common with modern-day gay marriages than any other relationships depicted in the Old Testament. It is extremely significant to note, therefore, that the Bible contains not the slightest hint of a negative judgment about either of these relationships. It never seems to occur to the biblical writers that the condemnations contained in Leviticus would have any application to cases like these.

I was finding that the results of my Old Testament survey were absolutely consistent with my conclusions about the purposes of God for marriage and sexuality. When the Old Testament depicts same-gender activity that is obviously incompatible with God's intention of forming people in self-giving love and mutuality, the passages always include a very negative judgment. In situations where a same-gender relationship appears fully capable of nurturing participants in self-giving love, no negative judgment appears. I was extremely heartened to find that my discoveries about God's purposes were making sense, even regarding the fragment passages that stand behind traditional condemnations. Reading such passages in their biblical and historical context allowed me to understand and affirm their judgments against violent and idolatrous sexual behaviors, without in any way compromising the positive conclusions I had come to regarding loving, faithful same-sex relationships.

CHAPTER 7

⬿⬿

RECLAIMING
THE WITNESSES 2

*Making Sense of the
New Testament Fragments*

I am teaching an introductory theology class, and the topic for the day is the Doctrine of God. I have been speaking for only a few minutes when one of the seminarians raises his hand, looking a bit sheepish. "Dr. Achtemeier," he says, "I know I'm not supposed to ask this, but isn't the God of the Old Testament pretty much completely different from the God of the New? I mean, the Old Testament God just seems really mean and wrathful sometimes, while the New Testament God is gracious and loving and forgiving. Aren't Christians really just talking about the New Testament when they speak about God?" I look around and see heads nodding all over the room. "That's why I never preach from the Old Testament," chimes in another student. More murmurs of approval. I take a deep breath and start to explain as respectfully as I can that this is an understandable view, which has been held by many devout and well-meaning Christians across the centuries. The early church considered it very carefully, however, and concluded it was too much at odds with Jesus' teaching and the apostolic witness to qualify as acceptable Christian teaching. I note many of the students scribbling rapidly in their notebooks as we continue with the lecture.

I was feeling very good about the light my studies had shed on the Old Testament fragment passages. I had begun my work thinking these were categorical condemnations of gay people and instead found that they were reasonable and understandable judgments directed against awful behaviors that any sensible person would disapprove. I found I could wholeheartedly support the message of these passages without qualifying, in the least, my positive conclusions about gay marriage.

I knew that being able to account for the Old Testament fragments was not enough, however. Most ordinary Christians I knew put a great deal more stock in the witness of the New Testament than the Old. If I didn't find similarly positive results with the New Testament fragments, the work I had done on the Old Testament wouldn't carry much weight.

The four New Testament fragments that have been used to justify traditional condemnations of gay and lesbian people are Jude 5–7; Romans 1:18–27; 1 Corinthians 6:9–10; and 1 Timothy 1:10. My challenge, once again, would be to figure out exactly what kinds of same-gender behaviors these passages refer to. It felt that I had a head start in answering those questions, though, because the New Testament writers were all deeply influenced by the Old Testament. It seemed a good bet that a lot of the assumptions about same-gender behavior that I had uncovered in the Old Testament would carry over into the New.

Jude 5–7

I found my assumption about the influence of the Old Testament confirmed when one of the New Testament fragments made explicit reference back to the Sodom and Gomorrah story:

Sodom and Gomorrah and the surrounding cities, which . . .
indulged in sexual immorality and pursued unnatural lust,
serve as an example by undergoing a punishment of eternal
fire.

(Jude 7)

Though the judgment in this passage sounds very harsh, I
reminded myself that I could fully endorse and support the
judgment contained in the Sodom story. The same-sex activity
in the Sodom story was the attempted gang rape of foreigners,
and I had found that I agreed wholeheartedly with the Bible's
condemnation of it.

The writer of Jude does appear to introduce a new twist
to our understanding of the Sodom story, however. The literal
translation of the Greek in verse 7, which describes the sexual
lust involved in the gang rape, charges the men of Sodom with
"going after strange flesh."[1] This may be a reference to the fact
that the foreigners the mob wanted to rape were not human
males at all; they were *angels*. This interpretation is rendered
more likely by the fact that the preceding verse speaks about
angels coming down to earth. It may be that the writer of Jude
views the problem in Sodom not as violence and aggression
between persons of the same gender but as attacks across spe-
cies! This understanding would reflect an ancient tradition of
Bible interpretation dating from the time between the writing of
the Old and New Testaments.[2]

Whether or not the Jude passage refers to sexual aggression against angels, it clearly understands the threatened violence in the Sodom story as the product of a lust that has spun
completely out of control. This is important for understanding
the background of all the New Testament references to same-
gender behavior.

Neither the Old nor New Testament writers have any concept of sexual orientation. This means that when the biblical
writers consider same-sex behavior, they can understand it only
as a deliberate rejection of fully available heterosexual options in
service to out-of-control passions like anger, lust, or aggression.

This point is important to keep in mind if we are to understand Paul's discussion in Romans 1.[3]

The Biblical Context of Romans 1:18–27

The first chapter of Paul's letter to the Romans contains the most extensive reference to same-sex behaviors in the New Testament:

> Therefore God gave them up in the lusts of their hearts to impurity, to the degrading of their bodies among themselves, because they exchanged the truth about God for a lie and worshiped and served the creature rather than the Creator, who is blessed forever! Amen.
>
> For this reason God gave them up to degrading passions. Their women exchanged natural intercourse for unnatural, and in the same way also the men, giving up natural intercourse with women, were consumed with passion for one another. Men committed shameless acts with men and received in their own persons the due penalty for their error.
>
> (Rom. 1:24–27)

Correctly understanding what Paul is saying will require us to keep in mind the broader biblical context in which this fragment occurs. Paul's references to same-sex behavior appear as part of a larger argument that will conclude with the claim that, because all human beings have fallen under the power of sin, all human beings stand in need of the forgiving grace of God (3:21–25).

The reference to same-gender behavior occurs as part of a rhetorical "gotcha!" that Paul sets for his pious, Christian hearers. The apostle's challenge is to convince his audience that even God-fearing people like themselves are wholly dependent on the forgiving grace of God offered in Christ. Paul sets his trap by appealing to his listeners' prejudices against their pagan, idol-worshiping neighbors. Of the pagans he says,

> Claiming to be wise, they became fools; and they exchanged the glory of the immortal God for images resembling a mortal human being or birds or four-footed animals or reptiles.
>
> (1:22–23)

These verses introduce Paul's basic theme for the discussion. The Greco-Roman pagans have deliberately rejected the true God from the center of their lives (vv. 19–20) and have substituted creatures—idols in the shape of created animals and people—as the objects of their religious devotion. This perverse choice causes the rest of their lives to unravel as well. Their corrupted minds and hearts rush to embrace everything in life that is opposed to God's will:

> They were filled with every kind of wickedness, evil, covetousness, malice. Full of envy, murder, strife, deceit, craftiness, they are gossips, slanderers, God-haters, insolent, haughty, boastful, inventors of evil, rebellious toward parents, foolish, faithless, heartless, ruthless.
>
> (vv. 29–31)

We can almost hear Paul's audience murmuring their self-righteous approval: "Yes! These pagans really are stupid and wicked and awful! Preach it, brother!"

But at this point Paul springs his trap:

> Therefore you have no excuse, whoever you are, when you judge others; for in passing judgment on another you condemn yourself, because you, the judge, are doing the very same things.
>
> (2:1)

Paul's point is that in self-righteously passing judgment on their pagan neighbors, his pious hearers also substitute creatures for God at the center of their lives. Rather than allowing the true God to pass judgment, they have given free reign to self-righteous passions and taken on the role of judges themselves. In their righteous superiority directed against their pagan neighbors, Paul's hearers have exchanged the glory of the immortal God, the only wise judge, for the self-justifying judgments and prejudices of mere human creatures, namely themselves. In this way they are no better than their idol-worshiping neighbors when it comes to putting earthly, creaturely realities in those places where only God belongs.

Given this turn in Paul's argument, it is ironic in the extreme that so many Christians have used this passage in Romans *to pass judgment on their gay and lesbian neighbors!* In our zeal to pass judgment, we never read far enough in the context to see that this *is* a trap that Paul is springing. But Paul's point remains as valid now as it was in the first century. In condemning our neighbors, we put created beings (namely, ourselves) on the throne of judgment that belongs properly to God.

Although Paul's message against judging neighbors is clear, it is also true that he expects his hearers will react negatively to his passing references to same-gender behaviors. As with the Old Testament fragments, it is important to understand what kinds of behaviors Paul is talking about.

Paul's Historical Context

As in Old Testament times, the Greco-Roman society that Paul inhabited had no concept of sexual orientation and no cultural spaces or institutions that could support egalitarian, committed, same-sex relationships based on mutual love.[4] Publicly prominent same-gender behaviors in New Testament times would have been violent or exploitative: military victors raped prisoners of war, and masters routinely took advantage of slaves of both genders as a demonstration of dominance over them.

Homosexual prostitution also persisted into New Testament times, practiced as part of pagan worship: the Greek cult of the goddess Cybele, known among the Romans as Magna

Mater, featured homosexual prostitution as part of its worship rites.[5]

Another influential form of ancient same-sex behavior was the Greek tradition of pederasty. This was a social arrangement in which young boys provided sexual favors to older men in exchange for philosophical training and social patronage. The pederastic system had its own peculiar set of well-defined conventions; boys around the age of twelve were seen as highly attractive partners, with their "prime" coming to an end as they became old enough to grow a full beard. Divisions between the active and passive roles were scrupulously maintained, and it was considered shameful if the younger, passive partner experienced any sexual pleasure or physical satisfaction from the relationship. Pederasty served as a rite of passage for boys of a particular, privileged social class, who entered into it without any consideration for what we would today describe as a person's sexual orientation. Ancient writers describing this system could sometimes speak of love between the partners, but only within the fixed structures of the pederastic system and never within a covenanted framework of mutuality and equality. There was no formal expectation that these sexual liaisons would be lasting, neither were they expected to serve as an alternative to heterosexual marriage.[6]

A final group of same-sex behaviors that Paul's hearers would have associated with the idol-worshiping pagans came from the Roman emperors. The shameless debaucheries of the Roman imperial household were widely known, with the depraved excesses of emperors like Caligula and Nero claiming victims of both genders. Paul's cryptic statement in Romans 1:27, about shameless pagans receiving "in their own persons the due penalty for their error," may be a reference to Caligula's assassination. Prior to his murder, Caligula had publicly shamed and sexually humiliated one of the military officers who would later lead the attack against him. Among the fatal wounds inflicted during the assassination were deliberate sword thrusts through the emperor's private parts—a "due penalty" corresponding to his previous crimes![7]

Assessing Paul's Argument

Whether or not we find this reference plausible, the outlines of what Paul is saying in Romans 1 are clear. Paul is not attempting to provide a nuanced theological-ethical analysis of all the different types of same-sex activity that are present in the ancient world; he is appealing to his hearers' prejudices. By whipping his audience into a frenzy of indignation against the godless, idol-worshiping pagans, Paul lays the groundwork for the trap he will spring in chapter 2, when he will accuse his hearers of likewise abandoning God by their own judgmental attitudes toward their neighbors.

The central charge Paul uses to bait his audience is that the pagans have substitute idols for the true God. At the center of their worship, the pagans have "exchanged the glory of the immortal God for images resembling a mortal human being or birds or four-footed animals or reptiles" (1:23). Paul continues to lead his hearers deeper into his trap by pointing out how this idolatrous exchange affects all of life, as the pagans cast off any and all divine restraints and allow their own creaturely passions to control their actions.

The same-gender sexual activities that Paul's hearers associate with their pagan neighbors are a perfect illustration of this substitution Paul is talking about. Lacking any concept of sexual orientation, the only category available to Paul's audience for understanding same-sex activity is to view it as the product of out-of-control lust. Paul's point is that these idol worshipers have made the same substitution in their sexual lives as they have in their worship; they have exchanged the ordering will and intentions of the one true God for the chaos of creaturely passions run amok.

What do we make of Paul's negative judgment here? I found I could agree with it! None of the same-sex behaviors that were prominent in the first-century world showed the least bit of promise in furthering the purposes of God for love and marriage. They were violent or sacrilegious or exploitative; they arose out of huge power imbalances or unbridled lusts. Out-of-control passions have no ability to foster the mutual, loving gift of one's whole self to another person in accordance with God's intentions. Paul was right; these behaviors, which his hearers associated with the pagan idol worshipers, were completely at odds with God's intended purposes for love, marriage, and sexuality.

I wholeheartedly agreed with Paul's negative assessment of these idolatrous and excessive sexual activities. And it made no sense to say that his negative judgment of these abuses cast a cloud of judgment over the covenanted, faithful same-sex relationships that are possible in today's world. That would be like saying that because the Bible condemns the sexual abuse of slaves, therefore sexual intimacy in marriage should be off limits.

Paul's logic in Romans 1 made perfect sense; if you remove the one true God from the center of your life and worship, your sexual life disconnects from God's purposes as well. That was a valid point, one I could agree with, and it seemed amply borne out in the particular same-sex behaviors that characterized Paul's pagan neighbors. But it had no bearing on the faithful gay Christians I had encountered in the present day: These were not people who were disconnecting from God's purposes; they longed to have God at the center of their lives. Their faithful, covenanted relationships were fully capable of embodying God's purposes for love and marriage. Paul's justifiably negative view of the idolatrous and exploitative same-sex activities of his own time clearly had no bearing on my conclusions about the ability of these modern-day, covenanted, same-sex relationships to align with God's loving purposes.

Natural and Unnatural

In the course of my study, I ran across one possible hitch in my conclusions. Supporters of the traditional condemnations have sometimes understood Paul's mention of "natural" and "unnatural" sexual activity (vv. 26–27) as a biological reference to the way male and female body parts fit together. If Paul's negative reference to "unnatural" behavior included every instance where male and female genders are not both present, then he would be condemning every possible type of same-sex intimacy, whether the setting was gang rape or a loving marriage.

Reading the passage in its historical and biblical context, however, showed that this interpretation was highly anachronistic, imposing modern ways of thinking onto the biblical text. It is as though we were once again finding references to Honda Accords in the Scripture!

In point of fact, Paul uses "natural," not in a biological or anatomical sense, but as a description of behaviors that are broadly in line with prevailing customs and expectations. For example, Paul uses the same Greek word to suggest that "nature" teaches it is degrading for men to wear their hair long (1 Cor. 11:14).[8] This cannot be understood as some timeless truth grounded in biology or human anatomy. Paul is thoroughly familiar with the Hebrew Scriptures and knows full well that in the ancient period of the Judges, Samson's long hair was a sign of his consecration to God's service (Judg. 13:4–5). The claim that it is unnatural for men to have long hair is a judgment made in relation to the dictates of style and custom in Paul's own era.

Paul doesn't even view "unnatural" activity in a consistently negative light. He claims that God acts "contrary to nature" in bringing non-Jewish people into the church (Rom. 11:24)! Once again, Paul's description of God's action toward the Gentiles as "unnatural" has nothing to do with biology; he means that God has acted in a way that goes beyond the boundaries of peoples' customary expectations.

So when Paul characterizes certain sexual behaviors as contrary to nature, he isn't referring to anatomy. He means that these are behaviors, governed by out-of-control passions, that have cast off both divine guidance and all the ordinary constraints on peoples' actions. Such a description fits perfectly the violent and sacrilegious behaviors that were the subject of the Old Testament condemnations, providing a strong indication that these are the types of behavior Paul had in mind. Relationships that were shaped and guided by

God's purposes and intentions would therefore be the exact opposite of what Paul meant when he called certain activities "unnatural." Loving same-sex partnerships have the capacity to grow into an ever-deeper faithfulness to God's intentions. This makes them categorically different from the sorts of unconstrained and out-of-control behaviors that Paul condemns as unnatural.

Romans 1:26 also contains a reference to women exchanging natural intercourse for unnatural. I wondered about this, since on the face of it I thought same-sex behaviors among women might include much less violence than was true in this era for men. Here again, however, understanding the meaning of "natural" in Paul's historical context helped to clear up misunderstanding.

Although early Christian writers and preachers frequently dealt with the text of Romans, we have no record from the first three hundred years of church history of any commentator ever understanding Paul's comment as a reference to female-female sexual activity.[9] Instead, the Christians who stood closest to Paul's own time understood this as a reference to women departing from the traditional sexual roles that Greco-Roman society imposed on them. That ancient, first-century culture was extremely patriarchal by our standards, and the accepted role for women was to submit to their husbands as completely passive sexual partners. Early Christian commentators consistently understand Paul's statement as a reference to pagan women who behaved more aggressively or engaged in nonprocreative sexual behaviors with their male partners, thus overstepping the bounds of their "natural" (i.e., expected) role.

I confess I had a bit more trouble affirming this particular negative judgment. Societal views of proper behavior for women have changed considerably since the first century, and one of the reasons it is important to read passages in historical context is to avoid mistaking ancient cultural prejudices for timeless, sacred truths. It seems clear that Paul's early hearers would have viewed such aggressive behavior in women as an example of people throwing off social, moral, and religious constraints and allowing their lives to be governed by out-of-control passions. While today's expectations for women are considerably different, I did find I could affirm the underlying principle that Paul's comment reflects. Turning one's back on morality, divine guidance, and societal common sense in favor of ungovernable passions is still a recipe for disaster, even if the forms such rebellion might take are different today than in the first century.

1 Corinthians 6:9–10

Understanding the background to Paul's teaching in Romans helped make sense of the remaining two New Testament passages that mentioned same-sex behaviors. First Corinthians 6:9–10 contains a list of bad behaviors that Paul says are incompatible with inheriting the kingdom of God:

> Do not be deceived! Fornicators, idolaters, adulterers, male prostitutes, sodomites, thieves, the greedy, drunkards, revilers, robbers—none of these will inherit the kingdom of God.

Included in this "vice list" are two Greek words, *malakoi* and *arsenokoitai* , which have often been understood as references to practitioners of same-sex behaviors. The second of these words occurs only very rarely in ancient literature, however. Not having other contexts in which to see them used together leaves their meaning somewhat uncertain.

The NRSV translates *malakoi* as "male prostitutes" and *arsenokoitai* as "sodomites." In Greek, *malakoi* literally means "soft ones," and *arsenokoitai* is a combination of the Greek words for "man" and "bed." The sense of this conjunction could be "man-bedders" or "bed-men." These same Greek words for "man" and "bed" also occur together in an ancient Greek translation of Leviticus 20:13, leading some scholars to suggest that the meaning of the word is grounded in that Old Testament reference.[10] Scholars have debated whether *malakoi* and *arsenokoitai* refer to the partners in a pederastic relationship or to male prostitutes and their customers or even whether they refer to same-sex behaviors at all.[11] For our purposes, the most important thing is to recognize that these words refer to behaviors that do not look like a marriage relationship and to keep in mind both their biblical and historical contexts.

As in the Romans 1 passage, Paul is not offering the Corinthians any kind of nuanced or detailed moral analysis of particular types of sexual behavior. His larger argument, which spans chapters 5 and 6, challenges members of the Corinthian church who are practicing an "anything goes" version of Christianity. Some of the Corinthian Christians have apparently concluded that because they are forgiven through the grace of Christ, they are free to do anything they want. This false teaching has progressed to a point where they are bringing the Gospel into disrepute, engaging in behaviors that are shocking even to their pagan neighbors (5:1). Paul reiterates a point here that he also makes in Romans 6; God gives us a clean slate and a fresh start through the grace of Christ so that we can grow in Christ-like love and goodness (5:6–8).

In the course of making this argument, Paul uses vice lists three times to refer to the kinds of bad behavior that Christians are called to leave behind (5:10, 11; 6:9–10). His intention is not to present any teaching about the contents of the lists. He uses them as illustrations, confident that his hearers will immediately recognize them as examples of obviously unrighteous behavior.

Paul's possible reference to same-sex behaviors in the last of these three vice lists makes perfect sense when we view it in historical context; the exploitative, cultic, and pederastic forms of same-sex behavior that were prominent in Paul's world were so obviously at odds with God's purposes that they fit the bill perfectly when Paul was looking for illustrations of patently unrighteous behavior. We don't need to be scholars sorting out the precise, best translations of Greek words in order to affirm Paul's reference to them. We recognize, along with Paul's original hearers, that the violent, idolatrous, same-sex behaviors prevalent in the first century are completely inconsistent with God's gracious purposes for love, marriage, and sexuality.

It would make no sense, however, to take this fragment from Paul's argument about our need to grow in faithfulness and use it to *block* committed gay people from entering into loving marriages that can actually help them grow in faithfulness! As we have seen, the committed, loving gay relationships that are possible today can serve as powerful instruments helping people to grow into Christ-like love and self-giving. This is what God intends the gift of marriage to accomplish. It is precisely this kind of growth into the image of Christ that Paul commends to the congregation at Corinth.

In short, when we read this passage in its proper historical and biblical context, Paul's argument in 1 Corinthians supports exactly the kind of growth into the image of Christ's love that any marriage relationship can foster, gay or straight. I found I could affirm everything that Paul says in this passage, while remaining completely consistent with my findings about the purposes and intentions of God for marriage.

1 Timothy 1:9–10

As in the 1 Corinthians passage, 1 Timothy 1:9–10 contains a vice list that is used as part of a larger argument. In this case, the larger point is that true Christian discipleship finds its guiding principle not in preoccupation with all the technical details of biblical Law but in "love that comes from a pure heart, a good conscience, and sincere faith" (v. 5). The author of the letter argues that the appropriate use of biblical Law is to restrain peoples' bad behavior, with the vice list serving as an illustration of this:

> [T]he law is laid down not for the innocent but for the lawless and disobedient, for the godless and sinful, for the unholy and profane, for those who kill their father or mother, for

murderers, fornicators, sodomites [*arsenokoitais*], slave traders, liars, perjurers.

(vv. 9–10)

Once again, this passage's purpose is not to provide original teaching or detailed moral analysis of items in the list. The author is using the list as a representative sampling of what he is confident his audience already regards as terrible behaviors.

The grouping of *arsenokoitais* with the terms on either side of it may be significant. The Greek word *pornois*, which the NRSV translates "fornicators," can also refer to male prostitutes. This being the case, the three terms "fornicator," "sodomites," and "slave traders" may constitute a collective reference to the sex trade that developed in the Roman Empire, using young boys who were captured and subsequently castrated by the military in conquered territories. What the NRSV translates as fornicators, sodomites and slave traders may in fact refer to the customers, victims, and profiteers who were involved in these horrible human trafficking operations.[12]

This possible interpretation serves as a vivid reminder that these vice lists are referencing same-sex behaviors that are totally different from the mutually loving, committed, gay relationships that are possible in today's society and culture. We can fully agree with the author of 1 Timothy in viewing human sex trafficking as a terrible form of exploitation that is utterly contrary to God's will. But affirming this has no bearing on our previous conclusions about the ability of loving, committed, gay relationships to fulfill God's central purposes for love, marriage, and sexuality.

Summing Up . . .

Looking back over my review of the traditional fragment passages, I was delighted to find that when I viewed these texts in their biblical and historical context, I could wholeheartedly affirm the judgments they contained. Any sensible person could agree with Scripture's negative stance toward the exploitative, violent, and sacrilegious behaviors that these passages had in view.

I also felt a great sense of relief in recognizing that holding to my positive conclusions about same-sex marriage was not going to require me to ignore, water down, discount, or explain away these portions of the Bible's witness. I was greatly encouraged by everything I was learning. At this point in my journey, I felt it was time to go back one more time and double-check for signs that I was indeed on the right track.

CHAPTER 8

⁓⁓

TESTING THE SPIRITS

How Do We Know We're on the Right Track?

It was April 1534, and the German city of Münster was in crisis. Inspired by Martin Luther's Reformation and their personal interpretation of the newly translated Scriptures, radical Protestant Christians had become convinced that Münster was to be the "New Jerusalem," standing at the center of Christ's imminent return. The radicals had seized control of the city the previous January, but now forces hostile to the rebellion had gathered outside the city walls, laying siege to inhabitants within. Amid the escalating crisis, a charismatic twenty-five-year-old tailor's apprentice named Jan of Leyden stepped forward to assume the reins of power.

Jan had little formal schooling but relied on spiritual revelations and his personal interpretation of the Bible to guide his rule. Following his heartfelt convictions, Jan gathered a council of twelve elders around him and declared himself the new King David, destined to rule over the entire world upon Christ's return. Gold and silver coins commemorating his messianic rule were minted and placed in circulation throughout northern Europe.

Within Münster itself, Jan decreed the common ownership of all property, burned the city archives where deeds were kept, and ordered his soldiers to seize private property for communal use. Following the Spirit's leading, Jan also reinstituted the Old Testament practice of polygamy and issued laws making it illegal for any woman to refuse a proposal of marriage. While the common citizens of Münster starved under conditions imposed by the siege, Jan and his sixteen wives lived in sumptuous splendor within the royal palace. Anyone raising objections to his rule was summarily executed. Jan of Leyden's "messianic" rule came to a grisly end in June of the following year, when disillusioned citizens helped the besieging forces to enter the city. Jan was tortured and executed by the invading soldiers, but his name would live on for generations afterward as a symbol of scriptural conviction running dangerously off the rails.[1]

Throughout the history of the church, there have been well-meaning people who received "spiritual" revelations telling them to say things or do things that turn out to be anything but godly. Already in New Testament times, the apostle John warned his congregations against assuming that everyone who hears a spirit speaking to them is necessarily in touch with the *Holy* Spirit:

> Beloved, do not believe every spirit, but test the spirits to see whether they are from God; for many false prophets have gone out into the world.
>
> (1 John 4:1)

One way of testing the spirits, of course, is to ask whether or not their message is grounded in the witness of Scripture. But this test is far from foolproof, as we saw in chapter 2. Ungodly actions and attitudes have sometimes resulted from misguided interpretation of the Bible.

This need to test the spirits weighed heavily on my mind as I contemplated the results of my biblical investigations into God's purposes for love, marriage, and sexuality. My study had yielded results that turned upside down my previous, negative assumptions about same-sex relationships.

Many different scripturally grounded arguments were pointing me toward the same conclusion: God desires to bless and sanctify same-gender relationships no less than heterosexual unions. This conclusion was not the product of a single argument or line of investigation. It was the product of multiple, biblically grounded arguments all ending up at the same place:

— Coming to know a number of gay Christian believers had helped me see how traditional condemnations created situations that contradicted biblical teaching about both the fruits of righteousness and the nature of God.
— My investigation into God's essential purposes for human love, marriage, and sexuality revealed that gay relationships could fulfill those purposes as well as opposite-gender ones.
— My survey of the biblical witness from Genesis onward strongly pointed toward God's willingness to bless relationships that departed from the majority pattern of male and female set forth in the Genesis creation accounts.
— I discovered a consistent witness throughout both Old and New Testaments to a God who delights in providing blessing outside the bounds of customary ways of doing things.

I had also discovered that the fragment passages that informed the traditional condemnations were actually directed against behaviors that were completely different from the loving, committed same-sex partnerships that I was concerned with. I found I could agree fully with the negative judgments in the fragment texts without altering any of my other positive conclusions about gay marriage. In short, my study of Scripture gave me strong reason to believe that God stands ready to graciously bless and affirm same-sex relationships in the same way that God bestows blessing on heterosexual ones.

Before I invested too much in this changed understanding of the Bible's witness, however, I needed to find some assurance that my conclusions were on the right track. I was aware that Jan of Leyden was only one of many episodes in church history when sincere, well-meaning Christian believers came away from an encounter with Scripture bearing messages that were disastrously wrongheaded. What signs or assurances could I find to indicate my own conclusions, which departed so dramatically from traditional teaching, were not equally misguided?

Making Sense of Scripture

I had realized that human beings created in the image of the divine Logos could reasonably expect to find God's commands to them understandable (ch. 3). For this reason, it would be a powerful confirmation that a particular interpretation of Scripture was on the right track if it was able to make coherent, good sense out of other parts of Scripture. It appeared that my conclusions about God's purposes for love, marriage, and sexuality did exactly that.

In light of the divine purposes, the whole, broad sweep of biblical teaching about marriage and sexuality started to make sense. The Scripture testifies to God's intention that love, marriage, and sexuality should help us grow more and more into the divine image. God's goal is that these gracious gifts should lead each of us more and more into the joyous gift of our whole self to another person in a bond of mutually self-giving, Christ-like love.

When we think about giving ourselves away to another in this fashion, our first inclination might be to think that it all sounds rather grim and self-sacrificing. But one of the deep secrets of the Gospel is that we human beings find our true selves precisely in giving ourselves away. This is our deepest source of joy and fulfillment, because it is what God created us for. Jesus assures us of it when he teaches, "For those who want to save their life will lose it, and those who lose their life for my sake, and for the sake of the gospel, will save it" (Mark 8:35; see also Matt. 16:25; Luke 9:24).

Reflecting on the Bible's guidance about sexual matters, I realized that it all seemed to be designed to foster and protect a person's ability to make an all-encompassing gift of self to a beloved partner in Christ-like love and mutuality. Activities and situations that promoted this possibility found approval in the Scriptures. Situations that hindered this possibility tended to be forbidden. For example, the reason sexual relations apart from marriage fall short of God's intention is that they involve only a partial gift of oneself to the other person. The full gift of one's body to the other person is reflected in the form of sexual relations, but the full gift of life and spirit, expressed in the form of promises and commitments, is lacking.

The rationale for the commandment against adultery likewise becomes clear. Extramarital relations divide the gift of one's self; only a portion of one's bodily and spiritual gift is given to the spouse, another is given to the affair partner. Every encounter involves a partial withholding of the self for another partner. In addition to the dishonesty and broken promises that are inherent in such situations, the ability of the marital relationship to draw partners into the total gift of self to each other is undermined.

In a similar vein, understanding God's purposes for love, marriage, and sexuality enables Christians to articulate coherent reasons for the traditional prohibitions on polygamy and polyandry—marriage to multiple spouses. This critique is challenging, because the Old Testament records the polygamous marriages of a number of patriarchs and kings, including David and Solomon. These practices are reported with no hint of a negative judgment. But even in the face of such examples, we can see how the negative assessment of multiple-spouse relationships in the later Christian tradition makes sense. Such relationships involve a division of the self that results in a portion of the self being withheld from each of the marital partners. Once again the complete gift of self to another person is undermined.

A relationship that mirrors Christ's bond with the church requires the involvement of whole selves given freely to each other in love and mutuality. This helps make sense of the strictures in Christian tradition against rape, which involves coercion or exploitation; sexual relations with children, which involve large imbalances of power among parties to the relationship; and incest, where the bond between partners stands in the shadow of preexisting family connections and power dynamics. All these circumstances undermine the possibility of mutuality, making it extremely difficult for a genuinely free and unhindered self-giving to flourish.

In short, recognizing God's highest purpose in giving people the blessings of love, marriage, and sexuality turned out to be a powerful tool for fitting the whole range of biblical teaching about sex into a single, coherent picture. On one side, Scripture supports behaviors that help people grow in the mutual, loving, Christ-like gift of their whole selves to another person. And on the opposite side, the Bible is very critical of behaviors that interfere with this divine purpose or contradict it. This is why Scripture holds such a negative view of the violent, exploitative, and idolatrous behaviors that stood behind the traditional fragment passages, as we saw in the previous two chapters.

Other Tests

Thus far my biblically grounded theory about the purposes of God for love, marriage, and sexuality was holding up very well. When it came to *making coherent, good sense* of the broader witness of Scripture, my understanding of the divine intentions yielded impressive results. This was extremely encouraging!

When I went to back to check the results of my study against other criteria for faithful interpretation (see ch. 3), I also found reason to be encouraged. My account of the purposes of God was *grounded in the "big picture"* that Scripture presents of God's will for humankind. It was the product of a survey of the broad witness of Scripture, rather than depending on a few isolated fragments.

The understanding of God's will for love, marriage, and sexuality I had drawn from the Scripture was also firmly *centered in Christ*. Indeed, I had discovered the highest purpose for love and marriage in God's plan was to form us in the image of Christ. Jesus' loving gift of his whole self for the church was the model and prototype for the kind of joyful, self-giving communion God wants us to experience in marriage (ch. 4).

My study had certainly made extensive use of the classical guideline suggesting that we ought to *interpret Scripture by Scripture*. To better understand divine intentions underlying the Bible's teaching in passages containing particular instruction about marriage and sexuality, I had drawn on the witness of many different parts of the Bible. Also, in passages that referred to same-sex behaviors in shorthand or summary fashion, I relied on parts of Scripture that contained more elaborate descriptions of such behaviors in order to better understand the kind of behaviors the summary passages had in mind.

Finally, interpreting particular Scripture passages in their proper *biblical and historical contexts* played a key role in coming to a coherent understanding of the whole witness of Scripture about marriage and sexuality. Understanding the historical context of the traditional fragment passages had allowed me to fully affirm and embrace their negative view of the violent, exploitative, and idolatrous same-sex behaviors characteristic of that time, without casting any sort of shadow over the positive conclusions about gay marriage that had emerged from my broader survey of the biblical witness.

In short, when I surveyed classical guidelines for faithfully interpreting Scripture, I found good reason to believe that my conclusions were on the right track. But there was one more question I wanted to follow up on.

Is There a Precedent?

It had become clear to me that in dealing with contemporary questions about gay marriage, the church was facing a new situation. In today's society, it is possible for ordinary people to live out a same-sex orientation by entering openly into faithful, loving, egalitarian marriages or covenanted partnerships. This possibility did not exist until quite recently, and it certainly wasn't an option in biblical times.

The Bible does present us with a consistently negative view of certain kinds of same-sex activity. But as we saw in our preceding chapters, these were violent and exploitative behaviors that any reasonable person would view negatively, regardless of whether they occurred in a same-sex or a heterosexual context. The situation on which the Bible is passing judgment are miles removed from anything resembling the faithful, egalitarian, gay relationships that are newly possible in today's world.

This means that when we rethink questions about sexuality and come to positive conclusions about gay marriage, we are not overturning centuries of established church teaching or undermining what Christians have always believed. Christians before the modern era never had occasion to deal with the possibility of gay people getting married—it has never before now been a socially available option.

So in thinking through the issues surrounding gay marriage, we are considering new questions that the modern world has placed on the church's doorstep. The Bible does not speak directly to the question of gay marriage one way or the other, because such a possibility simply wasn't on the radar screen of the biblical writers.

But because the Bible doesn't speak directly on this issue doesn't mean we can't learn from what the Scripture does say. There are a great many features of today's world that were never foreseen in the Bible, from issues of technology and media, to the environment, to global economic policy, to all the undreamed-of capabilities of modern medicine. When it comes to speaking a biblical word to newly emerging issues like these, the church has always gone back to what the Bible says to its own place and time. From these particular teachings we can extract more generally applicable principles and insights about human life in relation to God, which then help us to deal faithfully with modern questions that the biblical writers did not anticipate.

I realized this was exactly the procedure I had followed in thinking through questions about gay marriage. Beginning with what the Bible does say about God's purposes for love, marriage, and sexuality, I used these insights as the basis for recognizing that loving, committed, same-sex relationships are fully compatible with God's will and intentions.

I realized, however, that many people might not agree with my description of what I had done. I knew a lot of people who simply assumed that the Bible had always presented us with across-the-board condemnations of every possible variety of same-sex activity. I was attempting to offer a more nuanced view, suggesting that in the light of modern developments, not all same-sex activity could be lumped together under a single category. While the traditional condemnations still apply to certain types of violent and sacrilegious same-sex behaviors that were prominent in the biblical world, newly emergent possibilities for same-sex marriage need to be evaluated according to a different aspect of the Bible's witness.

As much sense as it all seemed to make, I found myself wondering if I was completely out on a limb with this suggestion. Had there been other situations in the history of the church where across-the-board biblical prohibitions wound up being nuanced and scaled back in light of modern developments that the biblical writers never anticipated?

The Question of Interest Payments

I found a striking precedent in the history of my own Presbyterian and Reformed church heritage. John Calvin, one of the founders of that tradition, faced a situation in the 1500s that revolved around biblical teachings about usury, the practice of receiving interest payments on loans and deposits.[2] Up until Calvin's time, the church had taught that the Bible universally condemned the practice of receiving interest payments on money placed in the hands of another person. This blanket condemnation was based on a series of scriptural fragments from the Old Testament. Exodus 22:25 is typical:

> If you lend money to my people, to the poor among you, you shall not deal with them as a creditor; you shall not exact interest from them.

Other Old Testament passages used in making the case were Leviticus 25:35–38; Deuteronomy 23:19–20; Psalm 15:5; and Ezekiel 18:17.

These passages clearly prohibited the Israelites from charging interest on loans made to one another. Deuteronomy 23:19–20 contains an exception for loans to members of other nations, but the church had always taught that Jesus overruled the exception in Luke 6:35: "But love your enemies, do good, and lend, expecting nothing in return."[3] Based on these passages, the church in Calvin's time believed that the Bible contained a prohibition against ever receiving interest for any loan or deposit.

The problem Calvin faced was that a changing economic system had raised questions about usury that the biblical writers never anticipated. Calvin's society was experiencing a growing need for commercial business loans. Well-to-do Christians were in a position to be able to loan money to aspiring merchants or businesspeople, who in turn could use such loans to build up their own commercial enterprises. Since everyone assumed the Bible prohibited paying any sort of interest or return on such investments, however, there was little incentive to make interest-free commercial loans outside the circle of one's immediate family. The biblical prohibition against usury was forcing a great many promising economic opportunities to go unrealized.

Calvin went back to the Bible, trying to gain a better understanding of this situation. To my great delight, I discovered that the procedure he followed in trying to faithfully understand Scripture sounded extremely familiar: Calvin worked to figure out the purpose and intention of God that stood behind the usury commands, and he also sought to understand the biblical teachings on usury in their historical and biblical context!

Calvin's attempts to read Leviticus 25:35–37 and similar texts in historical context led him to realize that the usury commands originally functioned in an agricultural economy where poor people sometimes had to borrow in order to survive to the next harvest. Taking advantage of their desperation by charging interest on loans would dig them into an even deeper hole, making it all the harder for them to sustain themselves in future years. From investigations like these, Calvin discerned the divine purpose standing behind the usury prohibition: "[W]e see that the end for which the law was framed was that men should not cruelly oppress the poor, who ought rather to receive sympathy and compassion."[4]

Calvin firmly believed that biblical teaching should make practical good sense. The usury prohibition was not just a rote commandment given to exact unthinking obedience from people. It was given in the service of God's compassion for the poor, which is also to be reflected in the life of God's people.

This understanding of the divine purpose and intention standing behind the usury command enabled Calvin to recognize that certain types of lending, which were newly arisen in his own day, had no bearing on the issues at stake in the usury commandment. The biblical writers never anticipated that people would one day want to lend money to already-wealthy individuals in order to help them make even more money. Such lending was not a form of oppression; it was a service provided to the borrower of the money. Calvin concludes that receiving interest for this newly possible type of modern loan was something completely different from the situation that the usury commands were condemning: "Whence it follows that the gain which he who lends his money upon interest acquires, without doing injury to anyone, is not to be included under the head of unlawful usury."[5] Calvin's judgment is still relevant today. If he had not reconsidered the prohibition on usury, we would all stand under biblical condemnation for receiving interest on savings accounts and other investments.

Calvin further argued that this new, modern type of lending needed to be evaluated by other parts of Scripture. The relevant biblical teaching for commercial transactions was not the prohibition on usury, but the basic principles of fairness and mutual benevolence, as exemplified in Jesus' teaching of the Golden Rule: "In everything do to others as you would have them do to you" (Matt. 7:12). If I do my bankers a service by allowing them use of the money I have put into my savings account, it is only fair that the bankers do me a service in return by allowing me to share in a portion of the profits they have made with it. This is why the interest payments I receive on my savings account are not in violation of biblical Law. We take such scenarios so much for granted today. It is surprising to find out that they are the product of Calvin's faithful reinterpretation of Scripture, taking into account developments in his own time that were not on the radar screen of the biblical writers.

Parallels with Calvin's Process

I found in Calvin's discussion of the usury prohibition a striking precedent for my own work with the Bible on gay marriage. Calvin in his day confronted a traditional biblical teaching that everyone thought involved an across-the-board prohibition on charging interest. Today we are faced with biblical teachings that have been widely assumed to provide an across-the-board prohibition against all types of same-sex relationships.

Calvin sought in the broader witness of Scripture to understand the divine purposes standing behind the usury prohibitions. He concluded that the background of the commands was God's desire to protect and aid poor people. We have sought in the broader witness of Scripture to understand the divine purposes standing behind the Bible's teaching on sexuality. We concluded that the background of the biblical commands about sex was God's desire to nurture people in self-giving, Christ-like love.

Calvin investigated the historical context of the usury fragment passages and discovered that the prohibitions were directed against loans that served to add to the burden of poor people and increase their desperation, in direct violation of God's purpose and intention to care for the needy. We have investigated the historical context of the fragment passages on homosexuality and discovered that the prohibitions were directed toward idolatrous, violent, and exploitative same-gender behaviors that directly violated God's purpose and intention of forming people in self-giving love.

Calvin realized that his own day and time had yielded the possibility of a new type of lending, in the form of commercial business loans and deposits, that the biblical writers had not anticipated. We recognized that our own day and time has created the possibility of a type of same-gender relationship, in the form of loving, egalitarian, same-sex marriage, that the biblical writers had not anticipated.

Calvin fully affirmed the Bible's teaching against exploiting the poor, while recognizing that the commercial lending of his time was not included in this negative judgment. He moved beyond the fragment passages to the broader witness of Scripture about justice and fairness in order to guide such activity. We have fully affirmed the Bible's teaching against violent and idolatrous same-sex behaviors, while recognizing that the loving, same-gender marriages that are possible today are not included in this negative judgment. We moved beyond the fragment passages to the broader witness of Scripture about love, marriage, and sexuality to guide such relationships.

In short, it became crystal clear to me that Calvin's conclusions followed the same patterns as my own. In light of new social developments in his own time, Calvin had limited the scope of a biblical prohibition that people had previously thought was universal. He did this in order to bring church teaching more in line with a clear understanding of the purposes of God. And almost no one questioned the biblical validity of what Calvin had done. I have not known any Christian friends to worry that they might be violating biblical teaching by putting money into an interest-bearing savings account! After spending time with Calvin, I was greatly reassured that there was nothing novel or suspect about the way I had sought to understand the Bible's teaching for contemporary same-sex marriages.

Summing Up

I was starting to feel very confident in my conclusions. The means I had used for interpreting Scripture were all grounded in the classical Christian tradition. The work I had carried out met the criteria for faithful interpretation. The conclusions I had come to made powerful good sense. They made it possible to draw together the whole body of biblical teaching about love, marriage, and sexuality into a coherent whole that made sense and lined up with the scripturally revealed purposes of God. In arriving at these conclusions, I had not found any need to ignore, discount, pass over, or declare irrelevant any of the fragment passages traditionally cited in these discussions. These fragments actually supported the big picture of God's intentions that had emerged from my work, condemning behaviors that were clearly at odds with God's purposes for love, marriage, and sexuality. Finally, there was rock-solid precedent in the Christian tradition, both for the way I had gone about trying to understand the Bible's teaching and for the type of conclusions I had come to.

The biblical case in favor of same-sex marriage was starting to feel overwhelming. I knew I could never go back to my old ways of thinking. The one question remaining was how to translate the insights I had gained into practical guidance that could help all Christians, both gay and straight, live out their commitments to Christ more fully, faithfully, and joyously.

CHAPTER 9

⸺ ✦ ⸺

THE WORD OF LIFE

*Biblical Teaching
for the Real World*

I was fresh out of graduate school and feeling a bit full of myself. I'd been asked to give a talk on "making ethical decisions" for an adult Sunday school class. I spent thirty minutes outlining and talking through a sophisticated decision calculus. My diagrams on the blackboard were truly impressive! After finishing this elaborate presentation, I looked and saw that an older gentleman in the back row had his hand up. "Well Mark," he said, in his slow southern drawl, "that's all really impressive. But you know, I don't have too many situations where my problem is figuring out what is the right thing to do. My problem is doing it!"

⸺ ✦ ⸺

The gap between theory and practice can be difficult to bridge. Our everyday experience of love, marriage, and sexuality can be joyous, heartbreaking, comical, frustrating, fulfilling, puzzling, consuming, sustaining, debilitating, tragic, ecstatic, dehumanizing, elevating, crippled by insecurities, or filled to overflowing with God's grace. Often it is many of these at the same time.

My work with the Bible had yielded an ideal image of what love, marriage, and sexuality should look like according to God's loving will and intention for human beings. God's purpose was to draw people into relationships of joyous, self-giving love and mutuality where they could learn to give themselves totally to another person according to the pattern of Christ's self-giving love for us.

Biblical Ideals vs. Real Life

The problem with an ideal like this is that nobody is capable of living up to it. Among my own circle of acquaintances, I had encountered a substantial number of happy, lasting marriages, and I felt blessed to be able to include among them my own thirty-plus years of marriage to my wife, Kat. But none of these relationships fully reflected this scriptural ideal of consistent, mutual love and whole-hearted self-giving. I knew my wife would readily affirm that there were many days when I personally fell short of being completely Christ-like!

Of course marriage and sexuality are not the only areas of biblical teaching where we encounter a significant gap between high scriptural ideals and the more down-to-earth realities of everyday life. "Love your enemies and pray for those who persecute you" is a daunting challenge for any of us (Matt. 5:44)! I knew that proposing a Christ-like ideal for marriage and sexuality that nobody could fully live up to would be a major challenge, even though it was thoroughly biblical. This was not the way a great many Christians were accustomed to thinking about sexual matters.

The Problem of All-or-Nothing Thinking

Most of the ordinary churchgoers I knew were accustomed to thinking about marriage and sexuality in black-and-white, all-or-nothing terms. Either you are fully in line with God's will, or you stand condemned. There isn't much room in such a view for ideals no one can ever fully live up to.

I like to call this understanding of discipleship "minefield ethics," because it makes Christian life feel a lot like picking one's way through a field of land mines.[1] In this view, there is one path of righteousness and blessing that we must follow through life. This path leads ultimately to heaven, but it is surrounded by hazards—rules, prescriptions, and long lists of "thou-shalt-nots" line the path on every side. Following this path is similar to walking through a minefield, because a single wrong step can lead to disaster. If we step off the path, if we trip over one of the rules, then everything blows up in our faces. We are bad people, God condemns us, and our prospects for eternity in heaven are seriously diminished. In this view of Christian discipleship, fear is likely to be our primary motivation for seeking to obey God. We are anxious to avoid the wrath and judgment that will befall us if we stray from the right path.

Although this view of the Christian life is quite common, minefield ethics are a poor fit for the message of the New Testament. For starters, minefield ethics assume that the standard pattern for the Christian life is following all God's commands, never straying from the rules, and remaining fully aligned with God's will. This assumption is very different from what the New Testament teaches. "There is no one who is righteous, not even one," writes Paul, quoting Psalm 14; "There is no one who has understanding, / there is no one who seeks God" (Rom. 3:10–11). Later on in 11:32 he says "God has imprisoned all in disobedience so that he may be merciful to all."

Jesus himself makes it clear that his coming will hold no benefit for people who believe their lives are fully in line with God's will: "Those who are well have no need of a physician, but those who are sick; I have come to call not the righteous but sinners" (Mark 2:17). Jesus' parable about the Pharisee and the tax collector amplifies this message, suggesting that the people who honestly admit and confess their shortcomings will find favor with God, even if their sins are grievous. People who are convinced of their own righteousness, by contrast, fail to win God's approval, even if their sins appear outwardly to be relatively minor (Luke 18:9–14).

While minefield ethics tend to concentrate on warnings and pointers and pep talks for keeping righteous disciples on the true path, the New Testament extends the good news of God's grace, mercy, and healing to lost and hopeless sinners through the cross of Christ.

Minefield ethics also tend to divide people into black-and-white categories. In the one group are the righteous faithful who follow the rules and remain on the path of blessing; in the other we find the errant sinners who stumble over the rules, stray from the true path, and stand condemned. This binary, all-or-nothing way of looking at Christian discipleship leads to serious distortions in the church's witness. Such a stance inevitably comes across as extremely judgmental: "We righteous church members have stayed on the path of true faithfulness and won God's favor; all those others who have fallen short now stand condemned." Such a view completely obscures the core proclamation of the New Testament, that God has acted in Christ to save *sinners*.

This black-and-white, righteous-or-sinners view of discipleship tends to lead Christians into stances of unrelenting negativity and condemnation as they speak to everyday situations that inevitably fall short of scriptural ideals. Furthermore, such negativity often comes across as hypocritical, because the people pronouncing judgment in the name of scriptural ideals rarely conform to them fully in their own lives. Maintaining the illusion that we are walking the path of true faithfulness will require us to either water down the teaching of Scripture or turn a blind eye to our own shortcomings. Unfortunately, one of the best ways to distract attention from our own failings is to focus zealously on the sins of our neighbors!

It was becoming obvious to me that minefield ethics fit poorly with the message of Scripture. This was good news, because such a worldview also fit poorly with the biblical understanding I had gained of God's purposes for love, marriage, and sexuality. A high ideal, which everyone strives for and nobody completely achieves, doesn't mesh well with an all-or-nothing view of life that says you are either completely in line with God's will or else you stand condemned. Clearly I needed to find a more faithful way of thinking about Christian discipleship.

God's Will and Human Desires

I found a starting point for a more biblical understanding of discipleship in the recognition that God's commands are given for our good. As we saw in chapter 3, God provides direction for our lives because, like any loving parent, God cares about us and wants to see our lives thrive and do well.

When I thought about what I learned about God's purposes for love, marriage, and sexuality, I realized that these divine intentions provided a picture of what such thriving looks like. Our loving God wants us to be able to experience faithful, loving, and satisfying marriages. God desires our intimate relationships to be a source of delight, support, and comfort that we can count on over the long term. God wants us to have the joy of knowing and being known, of experiencing ourselves as desired, and of desiring in return. God's wish for our closest relationships is that they help us grow in mutuality, self-giving, and unconditional love, bringing out the very best in us and helping us develop into the generous, compassionate, and grace-filled people God created us to be. God's desire for our sexuality is that it becomes the joyous, comforting, and satisfying physical expression of all the love, passion, and mutual desire that connects partners who are learning to give themselves completely to each other in the image of Christ.

Ideals like this are not alien to our desires for ourselves. Our popular culture constantly expresses longing for relationships that work and flourish in this way. The songs and stories that fill our airwaves celebrate people finding connections like this or lament the loss of them or chronicle the struggle to achieve them or give voice to our cynicism and despair at finding them out of reach. Striving to fulfill biblical ideals is not some unpleasant duty we struggle through to placate a divine authority figure; it is not some spiritual version of having to eat our brussel sprouts as children. No, God gives us commands to increase our chances of finding the sorts of relationships that we human beings already long to experience. The Bible's guidance represents God's road map for satisfying our hearts' deepest yearnings. It is in wholly giving ourselves away that we find our true selves.

One other key insight helped me find an alternative to minefield ethics, and it involved reclaiming the central message of the Gospel. In Jesus' cross and resurrection, God has redeemed us and reconciled us and forgiven all our sins. Our calling as Christians is to accept this incredible gift in faith and to live thankfully in response to it. This means that our acceptance and standing before God do not rise or fall with our ability to perfectly live up to any biblical ideal (a good thing seeing how we all fall short!). God's love for us does not go away when we fall short of perfection. To the contrary, a striking feature of Jesus' earthly ministry was the way he constantly reached out in love to "tax collectors and sinners"—people whom the society of his day regarded as morally unworthy outcasts.

A Field of Blessings

These insights suggested to me a very different picture of our life's journey; instead of a fearful passage through a dangerous minefield, it is a joyful walk through a field of God's blessings.

Each of these pictures shows a path through the field that represents the fullness of God's will for us. In the minefield picture, the primary motivation for seeking that path is fear; any misstep will bring God's condemnation. As we have seen, this fear is inconsistent with the Bible's message of Christ's love for sinners.

In the field of blessings, by contrast, sojourners are inspired to seek out God's path because of the rich blessings that await them there. The reason to strive faithfully after God's will in the area of marriage and sexuality is the deeply fulfilling relationships that such faithfulness makes possible.

Seeing our discipleship in this way also allows us to admit honestly that we are unable to live up to the Bible's ideals fully and consistently. None of us achieves perfectly consistent Christ-like love in this life. Our walk may take us nearer to or farther away from the path, but the field is such that we can still find blessing wherever we are.

Recognizing that limited blessings can also be found beyond the boundaries of God's ideal path allows for the realistic affirmation that our sexuality is the good gift of God. Making use of this gift in full accord with God's will and intentions certainly provides the richest possibilities for blessing. But finding ourselves a few steps off the path of Christ-like perfection, as fallen human beings inevitably do, does not instantly turn this good gift into something dark and poisonous.

This recognition can be difficult because we are so accustomed to minefield thinking in the area of sexuality—as though our whole life's worth and standing before God could be put in jeopardy by a single step off the approved path. For many of us, it takes deliberate effort to remind ourselves that God's commands are given for our good and that there is value in attending to scriptural ideals, even when we aren't able to live up to them perfectly.

Of course there are good reasons sexuality has become a charged subject for us, and these are bound up with the potentially serious consequences that accompany some types of sexual activity. We also ignore at our peril the deep and complicated ways in which sexual expression is bound up with our emotional attachments and sense of self.

The apostle Paul challenges members of the Corinthian church, who seem to be ignoring the deep connection between sexuality and emotional and spiritual life (1 Cor. 6:12–20). Apparently, some of the Corinthians are teaching that, just as food is meant for the stomach, so sex is just another bodily function that needs to be satisfied by whatever means are available. Paul responds by pointing out the deep connection that exists between bodies and spirits: "Do you not know that your bodies are members of Christ?" he asks in verse 15. Throwing our bodies around as cheap and insignificant commodities has a way of leading us to feel that our inmost selves are cheap and insignificant as well. Our bodies are closely bound up with our spirits.

The existence of potentially negative consequences, however, does not overshadow the larger point—that God's gifts of love and sexuality have the capacity to provide us with rich and wonderful blessings, even if none of us can fully live up to the ideal for them provided by Scripture. My remaining challenge was to figure out how God's ideal purposes for marriage and sexuality could work with this more biblical understanding of discipleship in providing practical and meaningful guidance for Christians in their everyday lives.

Making Use of an Impossible Ideal

Christians across the centuries have recognized the value in paying attention to biblical ideals, even when our chances of fully living up to them are remote. The theological tradition has condensed some of these insights into three "Uses of Biblical Law," which tell how an impossible scriptural ideal can help us even when its fulfillment is out of reach:

First, reflection on God's perfect will for us can remind us of our need for God's forgiving grace. Remembering how far short we fall from God's loving will for our lives humbles our spirits and subdues our pride. Awareness of our own shortcomings helps us to be more compassionate and less judgmental as we encounter the flaws in our neighbors. Most important, such reflection draws us closer to Christ as we come to appreciate how much we need the forgiving and healing grace that God offers to us in Jesus.[2]

Second, reflecting on God's ideal for our life can help us avoid drifting even farther away from God's will than we already are. Like travelers who are lost without a compass, our human tendencies toward rationalization and self-deception often lead us farther and farther away from the life-giving paths that God desires for our lives. Reflecting on the "true north" of God's ideal for us, even if we cannot live up to it fully, helps orient us and keep us from inadvertently wandering even farther away from the path.[3]

Third and most important, reflecting on God's perfect will for us can guide our discipleship and give us a goal to strive for.[4] As believers become more aware of God's presence and blessing in their lives, they find their hearts overflowing with thanksgiving and love for God. We want to be able to return thanks to the God who has given so much to us. Biblical ideals can help us understand what kind of gifts God truly wants from us.

This "wish list" from God is not arbitrary. As we have seen, our loving God asks particular things of us because God knows that if our lives conform to such patterns we will do well and flourish. We embrace this ideal pattern of life as best as we are able, not only as a means of pleasing God but also as the life-giving path that leads toward the best expressions of the joyful, thankful, and loving human beings God created us to be.

Minefield ethics knows only two questions to ask of any given situation in which we might find ourselves: Are we standing fully in accord with God's will? (We almost certainly are not, because all of us fall short.) Or are we standing under condemnation? (We assuredly are not, because God has redeemed us in Christ.)

In place of these misleading, all-or-nothing alternatives, the three "Uses of Biblical Law" give us the tools we need for bringing biblical teaching to bear in a helpful way on various life situations in which we might find ourselves. In any given circumstance, we can honestly ask how we stand in relation to God's perfect will for us. We can dare to answer this question truthfully, because we are confident of God's forgiving love that upholds us when we inevitably fall short.

Second, we can ask what dangers are inherent in a particular situation that might cause us to fall farther away from God's will and intention for us. What are the hazards or temptations inherent in our situation that we need to be on guard against?

Finally, in any given situation we can ask what the next right thing is for us to do. Without harboring any illusions that we are going to achieve a perfect fulfillment of God's will for us, what are positive, achievable next steps we can take to move us closer to the fullness of blessing that God desires for us?

The Joy of the Gospel

When addressing particular life situations, it is crucial to keep in mind the healing and forgiving grace that God has offered to fallen human beings in Christ. This grace is the constant backdrop of all our reflections. Eternal salvation is not at stake in these situations. Salvation is a gift, already assured in Christ. Rather, the path individuals choose in these and similar situations will help determine their ability to enter fully into the joy, grace, and fulfillment God desires them to experience. God provides gifts of love, marriage, and sexuality to gay and straight people alike, so that all of us may grow with a beloved partner into the deep joy of Christ-like love, mutuality, and self-giving. These gifts are one of the means God provides for connecting us with our truest selves as we grow into the compassionate, loving, and joyfully giving people God created us to be.

The church that is mindful of God's forgiveness and these possibilities for joy and fulfillment does not need to frame its guidance in terms of judgment, condemnation, and fear of punishment. Rather, this gospel joy allows the church to present its counsel as an invitation to enter into the full richness of experience, which is the divinely given birthright of God's beloved children.

CONCLUSION

Indeed, the word of God is living and active, sharper than any two-edged sword, piercing until it divides soul from spirit, joints from marrow; it is able to judge the thoughts and intentions of the heart.

(Heb. 4:12)

I find my heart filled with wonder and gratitude as I look back over the journey that has brought me from being an anti-gay church activist to the place where I find myself today. This experience leaves me in awe of the Bible's continuing ability to become a living Word for us; one with the power to address us in ways we did not expect, change parts of us we didn't think needed changing, and lead us to places we never expected to go. God has also blessed me along the way with a rich company of supportive friends, companions, and loved ones, and for that I am truly thankful.

Summarizing the Journey

The start of this journey found me realizing that something had to be wrong with the way I had been thinking about same-sex relationships. Though I mistakenly assumed that the Bible's message on this matter was straightforward, I couldn't ignore what I was beginning to see. The church's anti-gay teaching was causing massive spiritual alienation and psychological damage within the gay community, among believing gay Christians who struggled to conform their personal lives to the church's teaching and among the ranks of those who were driven out of the church altogether. The Bible strongly suggests that faithful church teaching and conscientious, committed discipleship should result in lives that flourish spiritually. Seeing instead the widespread spiritual devastation that flowed from the church's exclusionary teaching convinced me that something had to be wrong with the church's message and my own beliefs. I was not able to say at first what the problem was, so I turned to the pages of Scripture to find out.

Major support for the traditional condemnations of homosexuality derives from seven passages scattered throughout the biblical text, all of which express a negative judgment about some kind of same-sex activity. I knew enough church history to realize that teachings stitched together from biblical fragments in this way have not always proven faithful or reliable. Because of this I realized that an accurate review of the Bible's teaching on this subject needed to draw from the broad sweep of biblical teaching on love, marriage, and sexuality. I found a promising entry into this broader scriptural witness by asking what God's purposes and intentions were in entrusting these gifts to human beings.

Surveying the Bible with this question in mind revealed God's intention that marriage and sexuality should function to nurture people's growth into the image of God. The complete gift of body, life, and spirit in a relationship of mutual love and commitment with a beloved partner reflects growth into the image of Christ's self-giving love. It is precisely through giving ourselves away in this fashion that human beings find our true selves.

This divinely intended growth in self-giving is as much a possibility in same-sex relationships as it is in heterosexual ones. This naturally led to the conclusion that same-sex relationships have as much potential to be aligned with God's will as do heterosexual ones.

I wondered if there were other essential purposes for marriage that were bound up with capabilities—like biological procreation—that are available only in heterosexual relationships. I found no biblical evidence to suggest that these heterosexual-only capabilities were ever treated as essential features for a marriage to be considered valid in God's eyes. My conclusion, that same-sex marriages could be fully in tune with God's will and intentions, continued to look strong.

Questioning my results from another angle, I recognized that the creation stories in Genesis describe the union of male and female as a standard pattern for human life. I wondered if this counted as evidence against my conclusion that same-sex relationships could be aligned with God's will.

Surveying the Bible again, I found overwhelming evidence of God's willingness to provide blessing in situations that departed from standard patterns and expectations, including those set down as part of the original creation. There was nothing in Scripture to suggest that the standard pattern of male and female was a necessary requirement for the fulfillment of God's will and the experience of God's blessing. This finding added further weight to the biblical evidence supporting same-sex relationships.

I next turned my attention to the seven biblical fragments used to support the traditional condemnations. Reading these passages in their proper historical and biblical context, I discovered that the social and cultural settings of the biblical writers did not allow for the possibility of the sort of covenanted, faithful, egalitarian, gay partnerships and marriages that are available today. The negative judgments reflected in the biblical fragments were all directed against other types of activity, generally violent, exploitative, and idolatrous same-sex behaviors that were prominent in the biblical world. Some of the fragment texts provided detailed descriptions of the same-sex behaviors they were condemning. In such cases, the descriptions were always of violent, appalling conduct, confirming that these were the sorts of same-sex activities that the biblical writers had in view.

Once their historical context became clear, I found that I could fully embrace the negative judgments contained in the fragment texts. These negative judgments were still valid and still applied fully to the kinds of violent and idolatrous same-sex behaviors that were the historical targets of their disapproval.

But I also realized that modern social developments had made possible a new kind of loving, committed, egalitarian, same-sex relationship that the biblical writers never envisioned. I learned that in considering the question of today's same-sex marriages and covenanted partnerships, I was not overturning the judgments of the fragment texts. Rather, I was using established biblical principles to think through a genuinely new situation that the fragment texts never envisioned. The established principles in this case were God's revealed purposes for love, marriage, and sexuality. And it turned out that same-sex relationships could fulfill God's purposes every bit as well as heterosexual ones.

I further found that my conclusions about the purposes of God allowed me to make coherent sense of both the fragment texts and the broad sweep of the Bible's commandments relating to love, marriage, and sexuality. In situations that allowed for the possibility of growth in Christ-like love and self-giving, the Bible's witness was supportive. In situations that closed off or undermined the possibility of such growth, the Bible responded with warnings, condemnations, or prohibitions. This ability of my conclusions to take the whole body of biblical witness about sexuality and marriage and draw it together into a coherent, unified whole provided strong confirmation that my results were on the right track.

I finished my investigation by exploring how this knowledge of God's purposes could provide practical guidance and wisdom for real-world relationships, both gay and straight. I was pleased to discover that such guidance could take the form of a positive invitation to experience ever greater measures of joy, grace, and fulfillment as we live into the possibilities of self-giving love and mutuality that God sets before us, regardless of our sexual orientation.

The Road Ahead . . .

At this point in my journey, I find that the biblical case in support of gay marriage is overwhelming. As I hope this study has shown, the case for gay marriage is grounded in multiple, mutually reinforcing scriptural arguments, that together take into account the broad sweep of the Bible's witness. Support for same-sex relationships does not require discounting, overlooking, or ignoring any portion of the Scripture; it simply requires an accurate understanding of the Bible's witness.

At the same time that I have followed the path of this biblical journey, I have also become increasingly aware of the enormous toll that is being exacted, in the form of shattered lives and devastated spirits, as so many branches of the church cling stubbornly to the traditional condemnations. I think about all the alienated LGBT children of God, whose lives have been so broken by the church's confused proclamations, tragic misunderstandings, and occasional, outright malevolence. I find myself longing for the day when all who condemn and all who suffer will once again hear the clear voice of the gospel reaching out to bring healing and redemption in the midst of heartbreak and spiritual devastation. God's Word really is for them; the gospel is for them; Christ's love is for them; God's gifts of marriage and love and sexuality are *for them*. And the church of Jesus Christ needs to be for them, too. Biblical faithfulness requires it.

NOTES

Introduction

1. P. Mark Achtemeier, "The Upward Call of God: Submitting Our Sexuality to the Lordship of Christ," *Theology Matters* 2, no. 5 (September/October 1996): 1–7, accessed February 13, 2014, http://www.theologymatters.com/SEPOCT96.PDF.

2. Unless the context indicates otherwise, I will use the term "gay" throughout this work as an inclusive term referring to all persons, male and female, who have a sexual orientation toward the same gender.

3. Mark Achtemeier, "Springs in the Desert: Ordination Sermon for Scott Anderson" (sermon, Covenant Presbyterian Church, Madison, Wisconsin, October 8, 2011), accessed February 13, 2014, http://covnetpres.org/2011/10/ordination-sermon-for-scott-anderson/.

4. Adelle M. Banks, "Study: Youth See Christians as Judgmental, Anti-Gay," *USA Today*, October 10, 2007, accessed February 13, 2014, http://usatoday30.usatoday.com/news/religion/2007-10-10-christians-young_N.htm?loc=interstitialskip&partnerID=1660.

Chapter 1: The Harvest of Despair

1. Eberhard Bethge, *Dietrich Bonhoeffer: A Biograph*, rev. ed. (Minneapolis: Augsburg Fortress, 2000), 918; quoted in Eric Metaxas, *Bonhoeffer: Pastor, Martyr, Prophet, Spy* (Nashville: Thomas Nelson, 2010), 532.

2. Thomas H. Stahel, "I'm Here: An Interview with Andrew Sullivan," America, May 8, 1993, copyright © 1993 Andrew Sullivan, accessed July 23, 2013, http://sullivanarchives.theatlantic.com/interviews.php.artnum-19930508.html#.

3. Mark Achtemeier, "The Holiness of Christ: An Address to the National Celebration of Confessing Churches" (address, Confessing Churches Celebration, Atlanta, Georgia, February 26, 2002), reprinted in *A Cry of Need and Joy: Confessing the Faith in a New Millenium*, ed. Richard Burnett, vol. 1, (Lenoir, NC: Reformation Press, 2002), ch. 11.

4. Doug Stanglin, "Ministry Apologizes for Gay 'Cure' Program, Closes," *USA Today*, June 20, 2013, accessed July 23, 2013, http://www.usatoday.com/story/news/nation/2013/06/20/exodus-international-ministry-gay-converts-apologizes-closes/2441363/.

5. Catechism of the Catholic Church, §2358, accessed June 23, 2013, http://www.vatican.va/archive/ENG0015/__P85.HTM.

6. For a sample introduction to these discussions, see Heiko Oberman, "Wedded Bliss and World Peace: In Defiance of the Devil," in *Luther: Man between God and the Devil* (New Haven: Yale University Press, 1982), ch. 10. See also Steven Ozment, "Marriage and the Ministry in the Protestant Churches," in *The Age of Reform: 1250–1550* (New Haven: Yale University Press, 1980), ch.12.

7. See, e.g., Martin Luther, The Large Catechism, §213, accessed July 27, 2013, http://bookofconcord.org/lc-3-tencommandments.php#para213.

8. See, e.g., Martin Luther, "An Exhortation to the Knights of the Teutonic Order That They Lay Aside False Chastity and Assume the True Chastity of Wedlock," in Theodore G. Tappert, ed. *Selected Writings of Martin Luther, 1523-1526* (Philadelphia: Fortress Press, 1967), ch. 1.

9. See, e.g., John Calvin, *Institutes of the Christian Religion*, 4.13.3, 17; ed. John T. McNeill, trans. Ford Lewis Battles, LCC (Philadelphia: Westminster Press, 1955).

10. Calvin, *Institutes*, 2.8.42.

Chapter 2: Jesus and the Law

1. A helpful overview of some of these episodes can be found in Jack Rogers, *Jesus, the Bible, and Homosexuality* (Louisville, KY: Westminster John Knox Press, 2006), ch. 2.

2. The passages are Genesis 19:1–29; Judges 19:1–30; Leviticus 18:22 and 20:13; Jude 5–7; Romans 1:18–27; 1 Corinthians 6:9–10; and 1 Timothy 1:10.

Chapter 3: With All Your Mind

1. This is the modern-day designation of the city. In the time of Pothinus, the city was known as Lugundum, situated in Roman Gaul.

2. Irenaeus, *Against Heresies* 3.3.4, in Alexander Roberts and James Donaldson, eds., *Ante-Nicene Fathers: Volume 1*, accessed August 5, 2013, http://www.ccel.org/ccel/schaff/anf01.ix.iv.iv.html.

3. Irenaeus, *Against Heresies* 1.8.1, http://www.ccel.org/ccel/schaff/anf01.ix.ii.ix.html

4. A good overview of these principles may be found in two study papers, "Presbyterian Understanding and Use of Holy Scripture" and "Biblical Authority and Interpretation," issued by the predecessor denominations of the Presbyterian Church (U.S.A.). They are presently distributed by the PC(USA) as a single download and may be accessed at http://www.pcusa.org/resource/presbyterian-understanding-and-use-holy-scripture/.

5. Within the Hebrew Scriptures, the so-called "Ceremonial Law" might also strike modern readers as a set of essentially arbitrary regulations. An example of this would be the specifications for the design of the Tabernacle and its ceremonies in Exodus 25–29. But it was precisely in the conviction that this witness of Scripture was *not* arbitrary that the early church developed a thoroughgoing system for interpreting all such scriptural details as signs, types, and prophetic symbols pointing ahead to Christ. Luke attributes the origins of this project to the risen Christ himself (Luke 24:27).

6. The "arbitrary rules" approach to ethics I am describing is sometimes referred to in scholarly literature as the "ethics of taboo."

7. Tim Challies, "We Are All Virgins Now," July 25, 2013, accessed August 6, 2013, http://www.challies.com/articles/we-are-all-virgins-now.

8. Ibid., para. 3.

9. Ibid., para. 6.

10. Calvin, *Institutes*, 2.8.8; see also 2.8.6–10. "It [the Law] is to be . . . interpreted with reference to the purpose of the Lawgiver."

Chapter 4: "This Is My Body, Given for You"

1. See Paul Evdokimov, *The Sacrament of Love: The Nuptial Mystery in the Light of Orthodox Tradition,* trans. Anthony P. Gythiel and Victoria Steadman (Crestwood, NY: St. Vladimir's Seminary Press, 2001), 134-42, 154–57.

2. Paul's discussion in Corinthians was influenced by his hopeful but mistaken belief that Jesus was going to return within a very short period of time. This led him to conclude that Christians would be better off focusing their attention on Jesus' imminent return rather than getting involved in major life changes. But his understandings of marriage and singleness still come through clearly in the passage.

Chapter 5: Special Blessings

1. A more technical term for the argument from plumbing is the argument from Natural Law.

2. Jesus' teachings on divorce are intended to be life giving, and they need to be appropriated in the same manner as other expressions of biblical law. See the discussion in chapter 2 above.

3. For the sake of clarity, I am leaving out of the discussion the small, but significant, percentage of human beings who are born with anatomy that is indeterminately male or female.

4. www.gaychristian.net.

5. See Justin Lee, "Justin's View," The Gay Christian Network, accessed March 5, 2014, https://www.gaychristian.net/justins_view.php.

Chapter 6: Reclaiming the Witnesses 1

1. Martti Nissinen, *Homoeroticism in the Biblical World: A Historical Perspective,* trans. Kirsi Stjerna (Minneapolis: Fortress Press, 1998).

2. Ibid., 131.

Chapter 7: Reclaiming the Witnesses 2

1. Greek: *apelthousai opisō sarkos heteras.*

2. Nissinen, *Homoeroticism in the Biblical World*, 91–93.

3. For a very helpful discussion of how Romans 1 is shaped by Paul's understanding of same-sex behavior as excess passion, see Matthew Vines, *God and the Gay Christian* (New York: Convergent Books, 2014), 106–9.

4. For a more detailed discussion of this point, see Nissinen, *Homoeroticism in the Biblical World*, 128–32; also James Brownson, *Bible, Gender, Sexuality* (Grand Rapid: Eerdmans, 2013), 228–32.

5. Brownson, *Bible, Gender, Sexuality*, 243.

6. A fuller description can be found in Nissinen, *Homoeroticism in the Biblical World*, ch. 4.

7. Brownson, *Bible, Gender, Sexuality*, 156–59, citing Neil Elliot, *The Arrogance of Nations: Reading Romans in the Shadow of Empire, Paul in Critical Contexts* (Minneapolis: Fortress, 2008), 79-83. For a historical account of the assassination, see Suetonius, *The Twelve Caesars*, trans. Robert Graves, Penguin Classics Edition (New York: Penguin Books, 2007), "Gaius Caligula," §56–58.

8. The Greek word being translated as "nature" is *physis.*

9. Brownson, *Bible, Gender, Sexuality*, 207–8.

10. This ancient Greek translation of the Hebrew Old Testament is called the Septuagint.

11. For a detailed discussion see Nissinen, *Homoeroticism in the Biblical World*, 113–18.

12. Brownson, *Bible, Gender, Sexuality*, 274, citing Stacy Johnson, *A Time to Embrace: Same-Gender Relationships in Religion, Law, and Politics* (Grand Rapids, Eerdmans, 2006), 133.

Chapter 8: Testing the Spirits

1. See Diarmaid MacCulloch, "A New King David? Münster and Its Aftermath," in *The Reformation: A History* (New York: Viking Penguin Press, 2004), 199–206; also "Münster Anabaptists," in *Global Anabaptist Mennonite Encyclopedia Online*, accessed October 22, 2013, http://gameo.org/index .php?title=Münster_Anabaptists.

2. See John Calvin, "On Usury," in *Calvin's Ecclesiastical Advice*, trans. Mary Beaty and Benjamin Farley (Louisville, KY: Westminster/John Knox Press, 1991), 139–43. For a brief summary of Calvin's teaching on usury with illustrative quotes, see Daniel K. Finn, *Christian Economic Ethics: History and Implications* (Minneapolis, Fortress Press, 2013), 227–29. A more detailed treatment, which situates Calvin's thought in relation to the received traditions of Thomist scholasticism and Lutheran Protestantism can be found in Michael Wykes, "Devaluing the Scholastics: Calvin's Ethics of Usury," *Calvin Theological Journal* 38 (2003): 27–51, accessed December 18, 2013, http:// www.calvin.edu/library/database/crcpi/fulltext/ctj/88050.pdf.

3. It is worth noting here that the case against usury includes words from Jesus himself. This puts the prohibition of usury on a stronger footing than the traditional condemnations of homosexuality, which include no direct teaching from Jesus.

4. Commentary on Psalm 15:5, in John Calvin, *Commentary upon the Book of Psalms*, vol. 1, trans. James Anderson (Grand Rapids: Baker Book House, 1984), as quoted in Wykes, "Devaluing the Scholastics," 47.

5. Ibid.

Chapter 9: The Word of Life

1. A more technical description of what I am referring to would be a rule-based ethic that takes perfectionism for granted and ignores grace.

2. Students of theology will recognize in this description the first of the classical three uses of the Law, often called the Pedagogical Use.

3. This is an interpretation of the second, Juridical Use of the Law (sometimes called the Civil Use).

4. The imaginatively named "Third Use of the Law."

CPSIA information can be obtained at www.ICGtesting.com
Printed in the USA
BVOW08s1148160614

356494BV00001B/1/P